Feagour, Strathmashie.

About the author

KEVIN LANGAN is an experienced mountaineer and long distance walker who has a passion for exploring Scotland's wilderness areas. Kevin has spent much of his life trekking through Scotland's rich tapestry of hills and glens, as well as backpacking in the valleys of California and exploring tranquil Danish fjords.

With a track record for innovation in the outdoor sports industry, his portfolio of award-winning products range from collapsible climbing helmets inspired by the armadillo's folding armour, to tri-blade ice climbing tools inspired by the woodpecker's zygodactyl feet. He now specialises in conceptual planning and architectural design where he also found time to devise an award-winning modular hill shelter, expanding his portfolio of outdoor products.

The East Highland Way adheres to the same standards and Kevin has tackled the route with the same inventive methodology, planning strategy and attention to detail that are a hallmark of his work.

Advice to readers:

Before planning your walk visit **www.easthighlandway.com**
for any current guidebook updates or known route changes.

Enjoy Scotland's outdoors responsibly

Everyone has the right to be on most land and inland water for
recreation, education and for going from place to place providing they
act responsibly. These access rights and responsibilities are explained
in the Scottish Outdoor Access Code. The key points are:

When you're in the outdoors:

- take personal responsibility for your own actions and act safely
- respect people's privacy and peace of mind
- help land managers and others to work safely and effectively
- care for your environment and take your litter home
- keep your dog under proper control
- take extra care if organising an event or running a business

If you're managing the outdoors:

- respect access rights
- act reasonably when asking people to avoid land management
operations
- work with your local authority and other bodies to help integrate
access and land management
- respect rights of way and customary access

Visit **www.outdooraccess-scotland.com** or contact your
local Scottish Natural Heritage office.

(The East Highland Way is an unofficial route and involves some road
walking. Before your trip, please read the guidance established for
pedestrians in the Highway Code.)

The East Highland Way
Fort William to Aviemore

KEVIN LANGAN

Luath Press Limited
EDINBURGH
www.luath.co.uk

For Katie

Trekking and orienteering are not risk free activities and may prove difficult for some readers. While every care and effort has been taken in its preparation, readers should note that information contained within may not be accurate and can change following publication. Neither the publisher nor the author accept liability for loss, injury or damage of any kind arising directly or indirectly from the book's contents. The publisher welcomes feedback if any difficulties are experienced in interpreting the guide, or if route alterations or inaccuracies are noted.

First published 2010 by Sleepers Hill Publications, print-on-demand
Second edition 2011 with additional sections
Third edition 2012 with alterations and additional sections
Reprinted 2016 with alterations.
ISBN (10): 1-908373-40-7
ISBN (13): 978-1-908373-40-3

The paper used in this book is recyclable. It is made from low-chlorine pulps produced in a low-energy, low emission manner from renewable forests.

Printed and bound by CPI Antony Rowe, Chippenham

Typeset in Tahoma by Kevin Langan
Cover design & all graphics by Kevin Langan

All map diagrams designed by Kevin Langan based on detailed field surveys and notes taken between 2007 to 2010. Base information supplied by Open Street & Cycle Map (and) contributors (www. openstreetmap.org), and reproduced under the Creative Commons Licence.

Contents:

Foreword:

A number of years ago I followed an ancient route that ran from the shadows of the Cairngorms all the way to Fort William, a rather devious route that bypassed the main centres of population and remained fairly hidden. And for good reason. This was the Rathad nam Meirleach, or the cateran's road, and it was the trail used when cattle thieves from Lochaber raided the rich pasturelands of Moray. This was at a time when many of the western clans believed they had a divine right to lift the booty of the fertile Laich of Moray.

I've followed that route several times over the years, a route that traverses some wild and remote territory. I've walked it in summer and in winter and other than a couple of bothies, there is little in the way of comfortable accommodation. I've always used a tent, but I'm aware that many people today would rather use B&B or hotel accommodation on their long walks. That's the modern way, and with walking and backpacking being such big contributors to the rural highland economy there is also a need for long distance walking routes to pass through centres of population. That's why the East Highland Way will suit more people than the ancient Rathad nam Meirleach!

I like the idea of linking up the northern end of the West Highland Way with the Speyside Way, and I love the notion of a network of trails throughout the highlands of Scotland offering backpackers a choice of week long walks, two week long walks or even longer.

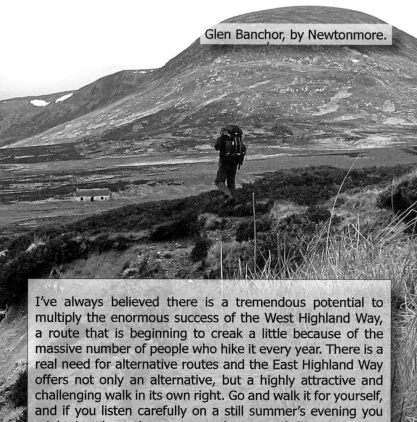

Glen Banchor, by Newtonmore.

I've always believed there is a tremendous potential to multiply the enormous success of the West Highland Way, a route that is beginning to creak a little because of the massive number of people who hike it every year. There is a real need for alternative routes and the East Highland Way offers not only an alternative, but a highly attractive and challenging walk in its own right. Go and walk it for yourself, and if you listen carefully on a still summer's evening you might just hear the groans and grunts of those sweating beasts being driven west to Lochaber by the freebooters of old.

Cameron McNeish, January 2011
www.cameronmcneish.co.uk

Introduction:

Scotland is a beautiful country, but it is not a big country, yet somehow, through a combination of varied topographies, history, culture and climate, it manages to convince us that it is. I have several times looked at two points on a map, points which are a couple of hours apart by road, and realised, with a sort of dumb astonishment, that they are only separated by about 20 miles of hill tracks. Surely you think to yourself, they've got to be further apart than that? They're not.

Aonach Mor

I once attended a meeting at Mar Lodge where one of Scotland's best known conservationists gob-smacked the assembled company by casually mentioning that he'd just walked there, across the hills, from the Rothiemurchus Estate. Folk looked at him as if he was the Jolly Green Giant. Now, don't get me wrong, it's a fair old hike but go and look at a map, it's surprisingly do-able.

This ability to ignore road networks and to look at a stretch of country and read it as a thoroughfare, a way from A to B, is increasingly rare, but Kevin Langan has it. Other long distance routes have been designed by committees, or government agencies – Kevin dreamt this one up by himself.

He has skilfully combined old drove roads, path networks and forest tracks and designed a route which not only passes through some of the most attractive and fascinating parts of Scotland, but which also links up two existing long distance routes, the West Highland Way and the Speyside Way. In theory, if time and midgies allow, you can now walk all the way from Glasgow to the Moray Firth.

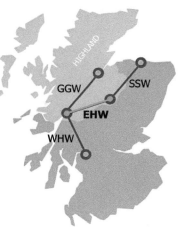

Route Key:
EHW – East Highland Way
Linked paths:
WHW – West Highland Way
GGW – Great Glen Way
SSW – Speyside Way

Like an army I tend to march on my stomach, so I like the fact that he tells you where to find a good bowl of soup or something more extensive along the way. He also flags up places to stay and where to find the odd distillery, this is all important stuff.

The East Highland Way runs through a rich seam of Scottish history – there's everything here from lost townships to pictish forts, Jacobite strongholds, the lair of the Wolf of Badenoch, Hanoverian barracks and what is possibly the most dramatically sited monument in Britain, the Commando Memorial at Spean Bridge.

There is also a lot of natural history – wildcat, red deer, pine martens, badgers, red squirrels, capercaillie, Scottish crossbills, etc. There are no guarantees obviously but it's always worth keeping your eyes open.

I think the genius of the book is this – Kevin Langan has not built one foot of path or set up a single signpost and yet he has single-handedly managed to devise a long distance route which should give pleasure and offer healthy exercise to thousands of people. I congratulate him on it, and bags I first go...

Mark Stephen, January 2011
Presenter, BBC Radio Scotland's *Out of Doors*.

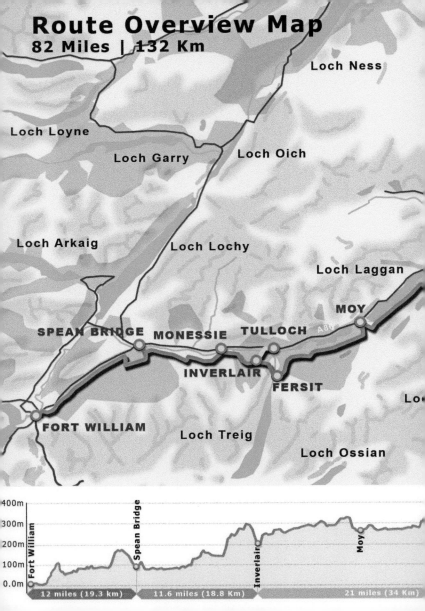

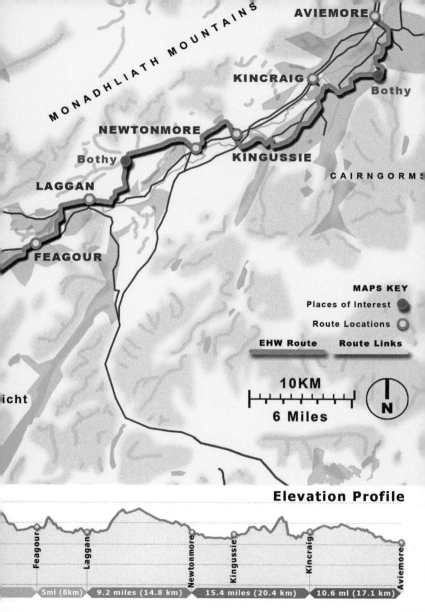

AVIEMORE

MONADHLIATH MOUNTAINS

KINCRAIG

Bothy

NEWTONMORE

Bothy

KINGUSSIE

LAGGAN

CAIRNGORMS

FEAGOUR

icht

MAPS KEY
Places of Interest
Route Locations

EHW Route   Route Links

10KM

6 Miles

N

Elevation Profile

Feagour | Laggan | Newtonmore | Kingussie | Kincraig | Aviemore

5ml (8km) | 9.2 miles (14.8 km) | 15.4 miles (20.4 km) | 10.6 ml (17.1 km)

Planning your walk:
1 – Following the way

Self guided route-finding can be a very rewarding part of any walking adventure. The East Highland Way is only waymarked through Ardverikie, Gynack and Badenoch unlike the official long distance trails, and as such the responsibility lies more with the walker to follow the route maps and written instructions within this guide. Route finding in this way has the added benefit of providing the walker with a real flavour of self-guided exploration. It's hard not to feel a huge sense of achievement in having successfully navigated a vast part of the country on foot, over a variety of landscapes. The countryside changes all the time, and although the maps and guidebook are as up-to-date as possible, you may encounter new tracks, recent forestry planting or felling, or other changes along the way. Before setting out on your trip please check the East Highland Way website for any updates or current route information (**www.easthighlandway.com**).

As mentioned, the route is not fully waymarked and it is important on various stretches to pay close attention to the maps and directional instructions, especially through dense forestry plantations where one will encounter various track junctions which have little or no distinctive features.

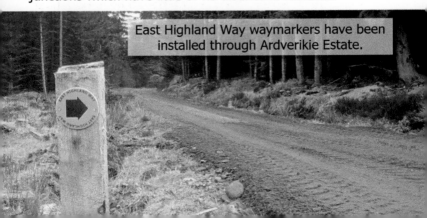

East Highland Way waymarkers have been installed through Ardverikie Estate.

Due to the visual density of some forested areas one can become easily disorientated, so care is required in these areas. Clear maps and instructions for passing through the plantations are covered in this guide and it is worth familiarising oneself with them prior to the trip, mainly for the Corrour and Inshriach Forests.

Some parts of the track do not appear on standard 1:50,000 OS maps. Firstly, the short 1.2 mile (2 km) stretch past the stunning Monessie Gorge at Achluachrach, where the route suggests you follow the River Spean eastwards until fording a small burn, proceeding through a timber gate and then ascending a plantation track. Although it may not be particularly intuitive or obvious underfoot, it is a special part of the experience, passing the old croft ruins of Achnacochine and crossing a historical fording point before entering a Narnia-like gate by some ruins on the opposite bank. In the summer months this can become slightly overgrown but really adds to the sense of adventure. Follow the river, cross the stream and you can't go wrong!

The second section, which is also less obvious underfoot (and may not appear correctly in OS maps), is the stretch through Balgowan and Glen Banchor beyond the Stalker's bothy. It's worth noting at this point that the footbridge which once spanned the stream by the stalker's bothy is no longer there. After some boulder-hopping one simply follows the River Calder eastwards along various eroded sandy banks and mossy sheep trails until rejoining a larger track downstream at the Newtonmore end. Again this is a very special part of the route, steeped in history, and in a wonderful setting. The scenic grandeur of the surrounding mountains helps make this part of the trip particularly rewarding, whether exposed in a complete winter white-out or baked in the hot summer sun, Glen Banchor is always a highlight.

2 – Times and distances

It is not possible to say precisely how long a complete traverse of the East Highland Way will take for any individual walker.

In this guidebook, the route has been split into seven sections of varying lengths and difficulties. Each section can be completed in a day's walk. By some margin, the longest and possibly toughest section is between Tulloch and Feagour. Here, the main route line heads south from Tulloch, passing the hamlets of Inverlair and Fersit. It then turns east as it skirts the south shore of the Moy Reservoir and Loch Laggan. This is a long day's hike even for experienced walkers, but due to the fairly level terrain and good tracks, can usually be completed without any problems. It is also possible to take a shortcut from Tulloch station to Moy Bridge along the usually quiet A86 which cuts out a good few miles from this long day's hike.

Walkers travel at their own speed, and performance will vary depending on weather, underfoot conditions and level of fitness. The table adjacent gives a general indication of how it is possible to walk the route in between four and seven days. The addition of deep snow can greatly increase walking times and the short daylight hours in winter can often push a day's walk into darkness. Always take head-torches when travelling in the winter months. The area is well known for its snowfall, as witness the towns and industries that have been established to exploit the winter sports market.

The Cairngorms National Park is Britain's largest national park and is renowned for its heavy snow in winter. The land above 600 metres – known as the 'montane zone' – is the largest area of arctic mountain landscape in the British Isles. From December to March, any part of the route could conceivably be snow covered, so it's well worth keeping an eye on the localised weather conditions if one is brave enough to be hiking in the winter months.

Naismith's Rule can be used to work out a very rough estimate for time and distance. This suggests allowing one hour for every 3 miles (5 km) to be walked, plus a further 30 minutes for every 300 m (1000 feet) to be climbed. Circumstances and weather can play havoc with this estimate and walkers are cautioned to allow themselves plenty of extra time.

In my experience most walkers should average 5 miles (8 km) in two hours. Many walkers can manage 8 to 10 miles before lunch (by walking for 4 to 5 hours), then a further 4 hours after lunch, averaging between 16 and 20 miles a day. If you're unsure as to how far you can comfortably walk, it is well advised to go for some long day hikes prior to your trip. Not only will this give you the opportunity to test your equipment but will also help you assess personal fitness levels and endurance.

Table 1:
Walking the route, 4 to 7 day schedule

Locations:	7 days:	6 days:	5 days:	4 days:
Spean Bridge	✔			
Achluachrach		✔	✔	
Tulloch	✔	✔	✔	✔
Feagour	✔	✔	✔	✔
Laggan	✔			
Newtonmore		✔		
Kingussie	✔		✔	✔
Kincraig	✔	✔		
Aviemore	✔	✔	✔	✔

(✔ – possible overnight stopping point)

Table 2: Distance chart

From:	To:	Mls	Km
Fort William	Torlundy	4.1	6.7
Torlundy	Spean Bridge	7.7	12.4
Spean Bridge	Achluachrach	6	9.7
Achluachrach	Inverlair	3.6	5.9
Inverlair	Tulloch	1.9	3.2
Inverlair	Moy Bridge	8.8	14.2
Moy Bridge	Feagour	12.3	19.8
Feagour	Achduchil junction	2.1	3.5
Achduchil junction	Wolftrax cafe	0.7	1.2
Achduchil junction	Laggan village	2.8	4.6
*Laggan village	Dalnashallag bothy	4.3	7
Dalnashallag bothy	Newtonmore	4.8	7.8
Newtonmore	Kingussie	5.8	9.4
Kingussie	Kincraig	9.6	15.5
Kincraig	Inshriach bothy	4.2	6.9
Inshriach bothy	Aviemore	6.3	10.2
	Direct Route:	**82**	**132**
Route options: ▮	**Overall Distance:**	**85**	**138**

* If the Glen Banchor streams are in spate during extended periods of wet weather there is a Laggan to Newtonmore alternative via Glentruim 9.6 miles (15.5 km). See p137.

3 – Route maps

The map diagrams within this guide have been specially designed to make traversing the route as simple as possible for experienced and novice walkers alike. The route is depicted as a clear red line with mountains in a buff colour, waterways in blue and forests green. Link paths from the main route to accommodation or attractions are shown as yellow lines. When used in conjunction with the altitude profiles, these diagrams can be useful in providing plenty of warning of rough terrain or steep ascents. The maps are depicted in a variety of scales depending on the particular section. Each section varies in length so be sure to compare the red route line with the corresponding distance key at the foot of each map which indicates the scale in both miles and kilometres. This should make judging distances and times fairly straight forward.

   Note that the East Highland Way website also hosts online Ordnance Survey route maps for each section, as well as detailed satellite imagery, accessible on-route via mobile devices should you experience navigational difficulties. For those who prefer to walk using physical Ordnance Survey maps, the whole route is covered in the following sheets:

OS Landranger (1:50,000: 35, 36, 41, 42)
OS Explorer (1:25,000: 392, 393, 402, 403)

Fort William from Loch Linnhe

4 – Packing checklist:

This equipment list is a rough guide; each individual walker's needs will vary. It has been broken down into essential and desirable items.

ⓘ Essential Items:

- Flexible **trekking boots** or sturdy **approach trainers**. Whichever footwear you choose, models with ankle support and a waterproof lining are always advised.
- **Hiking-socks**. Bring a fresh pair for each day plus some spares, as keeping your feet dry during the walk is important. They can also double as makeshift mittens during colder weather!
- **Waterproof jacket**. Most hooded, lightweight waterproof jackets are perfectly adequate. Consider using a chemical waterproofing agent on older jackets before the trip – available from most outdoor shops. Look for desirable properties like taped-seams, large pockets for camera, maps, phone etc. (Slightly longer jackets are more desirable as they can afford you the luxury of sitting down without getting your bum wet!)
- **Gaiters** for traversing boggy and muddy areas. They can also help keep boots dry.
- **Rucksack** with sufficient storage for all your needs. Look for padded and comfortable back support systems which often come in different sizes. A waterproof liner or cover is also essential. If camping, make sure your sleeping bag is wrapped separately in a polythene bag in case of heavy rainfall or accidental swimming! Use dry bags for any gadgets or electrical equipment that could become damaged through damp conditions.
- **Breathable clothing**. Take enough for your needs. Usually you will find that you require more regular changes of base layers such as t-shirts and undergarments. Outerwear such as fleeces and trousers tend to require less regular changes,

if at all, especially if gaiters are worn.
- **Water bottle**. Almost all Highland hill burns are perfectly good sources of drinking water. But please use your discretion or **purification tablets** if at all concerned.
- **Blister treatment**, **toilet paper** and basic **first aid kit**.
- **Guidebook**, **OS maps**, **compass and whistle**.
- **Insect repellent**. Expect midges from June to October.

ⓘ **Non-essential but desirable items:**
- **Camera**, **binoculars**, **mobile phone**.
- **Spare shoes / trekking sandals**. These can often be handy for bathing in the summer or just giving weary feet a rest in the evenings.
- **Sun protection**. **Sun block**, **sun glasses**, **hat** and UV **balm** for weather beaten lips.
- **Trekking pole**(s). Trekking poles can reduce compressive force on the knees by up to 25%. This translates into literally tons of accumulated load that your body will not have to support during the course of the route. They can also provide extra balance on slippery rocks especially when fording streams.
- **Pillow** (only if wild camping). A lightweight inflatable pillow is excellent and can help aid a good night's sleep. A household pillow-slip is a great alternative which you can then stuff with spare clothing.
- **Camping gear**. This varies drastically depending on specific requirements, i.e. budget, number of people, if you intend to cook evening meals, etc. Consult your local outdoor shop for tailored advice. A lightweight tent, sleeping mat and sleeping bag are the basic essentials. Refrain from starting fires in sensitive woodland areas along the route.
- **Spare plastic bags**. Having some shopping bags handy can be great for carrying wet clothing and waste, and indeed for keeping gear dry within the rucksack. In desperate times, they can be used over socks as a waterproof membrane if boots become completely waterlogged!

5 – Accommodation and facilities

For many walkers, good accommodation, shops and bars help transform a wilderness walk into a great holiday experience. The East Highland Way has been developed in such a way as to engage with accommodation and facilities where possible. At times this requires road walking: a necessary evil in order to reach these amenities. For those who prefer not to carry heavy backpacks, many tour operators now offer a baggage transfer service, accommodation booking and pick-ups. Local hotel operators will often arrange to collect walkers from accessible points via prior arrangement.

There are many bunkhouses, guesthouses and hostels along the route, not to mention fairly frequent shops, bars and restaurants. Knowing where these are located along the route is important, especially for those who may be wild camping or prefer to carry all their supplies. Check **www.easthighlandway.com/amenities.html** for a full list of current accommodation. The table adjacent indicates the various amenities and where you are likely to find them.

ⓘ **Booking services:**
Gemini Walks – www.geminiwalks.com
Contours – www.contours.co.uk
Easyways – www.easyways.com

Spean Bridge store.

Table 3:
Where to find amenities

Locations:	B & B	Hotel	Bunkhouse	Campsite	Wild Camping	Shop	Cafe / Restaurant
Fort William	✔	✔	✔	✔	✔	✔	✔
Torlundy	✔				✔		✔
Spean Bridge	✔	✔			✔	✔	✔
*Roy Bridge	✔	✔	✔	✔	✔	✔	✔
Achluachrach		✔	✔		✔		✔
*Tulloch			✔		✔		M
Feagour	P	P			✔		✔
Laggan	✔	✔	✔		✔	✔	✔
Newtonmore	✔	✔	✔	✔	✔	✔	✔
Kingussie	✔	✔	✔		✔	✔	✔
Loch Insh	✔	✔			✔	✔	✔
*Kincraig	✔	✔	✔		✔	✔	✔
Feshiebridge	✔				✔		
Aviemore	✔	✔	✔	✔	✔	✔	✔

* – Location close to the route, **M** – Meals available by arrangement,
P – Pick-up available by arrangment (see p113).

Historical attractions

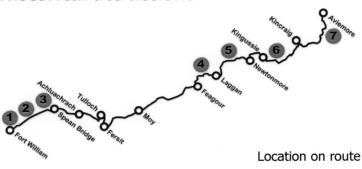

Location on route

1. Old Inverlochy Castle, Fort William, NN 120 754

The well-preserved ruin of Old Inverlochy Castle is regarded by some as being one of the most important strongholds in Scottish history. Its deep moat, not visible today, and strategic location banked against the River Lochy gave the castle a commanding defensive position in Lochaber (meaning 'convergence of lochs'). It is thought to have been built sometime in the 1200s on the site of an older fort which dated back another 500 years. It has been the site of two major battles: the MacDonald Clan's victory over the Stewarts in 1431 and the 1645 defeat of the Earl of Argyll at the hands of the Marquis of Montrose, followed by the massacre of the 1,300 defenders who were taken from the castle and put to the sword.

It is thought that in 1654 Oliver Cromwell erected a large timber-built citadel nearby which left Old Inverlochy Castle lying abandoned and redundant. This new timber fort was itself replaced by one of stone, named 'Fort William' after King William III. Fort William as we know it today, a town of almost 10,000 people, developed around the fort and was originally known as 'Maryburgh' after the Queen, Mary II.

Old Inverlochy Castle remains impressively intact. The same cannot be said for its successor 'Fort William', which was apparently destroyed at the time of the coming of the railway in 1866, with some stone footings being all that remain by the loch shore. In 1863 a newer Inverlochy Castle was built in nearby Torlundy, refurbished today as a luxury hotel. It is advised not to confuse the two!

2. Highbridge Jacobite Skirmish, by Spean Bridge, NN 199 819

The Jacobites were the supporters of the exiled Stuart king James II (Jacobus in Latin) and his heirs, who were deposed in the 'Glorious Revolution' of 1688–9. The Jacobite movement rapidly grew thereafter and was known to be strong in Scotland, Ireland and Wales. Jacobites offered a feasible alternative title to the crown under William III and Queen Anne, and several attempts were made to restore the Stuarts over the years that followed. In 1689, James II landed in Ireland, but his army was famously defeated at the Battle of the Boyne. In 1715, led by John Erskine, 6th Earl of Mar, Jacobites tried and failed to seize the crown for James Edward, the Old Pretender.

Highbridge ruin over a dramatic gorge.

In 1745, a further attempt was made on the crown by Prince Charles Edward Stuart, better known today as Bonnie Prince Charlie. When Prince Charlie first landed in Scotland, he met chiefs from Clans Cameron and MacDonald. The Jacobites again began to amass their forces. The Hanoverian governor of Fort Augustus sent two companies of Royal Scots, under the command of Captain (later General) Scott to reinforce the government garrison at Fort William. They were intercepted by a band of Jacobites at Highbridge (close to Spean Bridge). The small group of around 12, led by Major Donald MacDonald, managed to halt the advancing army by disguising their small numbers and using scare tactics. They then pursued the Hanoverians on foot as they retreated to Loch Lochy.

The government forces encountered more Jacobites who were strategically positioned on a hill to the west end of Loch Oich in an effort to halt the retreating army. In a last ditch effort, Captain Scott made for Invergarry Castle at Loch Lochy for protection. His retreat was further halted as the Clan MacDonell of Glengarry advanced from the opposite hillside. Surrounded and fatigued, they were forced to surrender, being told that any incompliance would result in them being 'cut to pieces'. Captain Scott's lone regiment had already lost two men in this skirmish and so surrendered.

Soon after, the Clan Cameron of Lochiel arrived to take charge of the prisoners, leading them south to Achnacarry. It is said that Captain Scott's captured grey gelding was presented to Prince Charles that day as he raised his standard at Glen Finnan. This skirmish marked the commencement of the fourth Jacobite rebellion of 1745, which eventually concluded with the Jacobites being massacred on Culloden Moor near Nairn by the advancing government army led by the Duke of Cumberland. (For a full range of information on the 1745 uprising visit **www.1745association.org.uk**.)

Memorial, Ben Nevis beyond.

3. Commando Memorial, by Spean Bridge, NN 207 824

Just north of Spean Bridge stands a 17 ft (5.2 m) high bronze memorial statue. It was unveiled in 1952 by the late Queen Mother after the sculptor, Scott Sutherland, won a design competition to commemorate the elite Commando soldiers who died during the Second World War. Achnacarry, (Achadh na Cairidh, meaning 'field of the fish-trap/weir') sited just a few miles from the memorial, was the Commandos' Basic Training Centre from 1942.

Over 25,000 men were trained at Achnacarry, including British, American and European troops. With a panoramic backdrop of north-facing mountain corries, this area was the perfect training environment to simulate extreme conditions for the Commandos. In November, wreath laying at the memorial is still an annual pilgrimage for many veteran Commandos.

ED · WE · CONQUER

IN MEMORY OF
THE OFFICERS AND
MEN OF
THE COMMANDOS
WHO DIED IN THE
SECOND WORLD WAR
1939-1945
THIS COUNTRY WAS
THEIR TRAINING
GROUND

ⓘ Scott Sutherland (15 May 1910–10 October 1984) was an award-winning sculptor born in the Highland town of Wick and schooled at Gray's School of Art in Aberdeen.

4. Dun da Lamh Pictish Fort, by Feagour, NN 582 929

Dun da Lamh Fort (Pronounced 'Dun-da-Larve') means 'fort of the two hands', which could be a reference to the two summits of Black Craig, from which the surrounding Black Woods also derive their name. It is considered to be one of the best remaining relics of a Scottish stronghold of its kind and is one of the most stunningly located historical sites in the Highlands.

The fort's walls are 20 feet thick in places and were skilfully constructed using high quality masonry, which is still evident today at the summit ruins. One source suggests that the 5000 tons of rock used to construct the once huge ramparts were not locally sourced and had to be carried from further afield. The fort is believed to date from around the earliest Pictish period. It is also thought to once have been a centre of power for the people who controlled the passes connecting Badenoch with the north, the south and the west during the later Iron Age (around 1500 years ago).

Stone remains at the summit.

Approaching Dun da Lamh from the Wolftrax café.

Local legend tells of it being built and lived in by the Fingalian Hunters, whose hill Tom na Feinne stands a few miles further down the Spey.

In those days, it was thought that Fingalian giants lived among the Picts. Of reputed Irish origin, these giants are common-place in Gaelic folklore (of Fingal's Cave fame). They were alleged to have possessed supernatural powers and in some cases to be romantically involved with fairies, although their size difference makes this somewhat difficult to visualise!

5. Glen Banchor's Lost Townships, by Newtonmore

Glen Banchor is a stunningly tranquil mountain pass between Laggan and Newtonmore. Flowing from west to east, the River Calder carves its way through the glen, eroding its soft peaty banks as it descends eastwards. The glen is apparently named after a long bend at the eastern end of the river; 'A Beannachar' meaning a 'horn-shaped' stretch of river bank.

Estate records from 1841 indicate 21 houses spread across various townships with a total of 85 inhabitants. Some fifty years later, the glen's 12 remaining inhabitants occupied only three houses. The once thriving population was cleared for more profitable sheep farming. This happened throughout the Highlands over many years and is known as the Highland Clearances. Eight townships can be found still marked on OS maps today and 19th century maps indicate a road or track reaching as far as the Dalballoch croft. This is nothing more than a boggy footpath today. Other than the odd ruined croft, the remains of this traditional way of life have been reduced to some stone rubble footings indicating buildings and enclosures of varying sizes spread throughout the glen.

ⓘ Replicas of these dwellings built from stone, turf and timber, can be seen today at the **Highland Folk Museum** in Newtonmore (p144).

The glen's displaced inhabitants moved east, building their new homes at 'Strone-muir' (meaning 'headland moor'), now Newtonmore, meaning 'New town on the Moor'.

Research suggests that people lived in Glen Banchor long before the cleared townships. Although not yet excavated, a one hundred foot long burial mound was discovered south of the river and a double palisaded enclosure (thought to be a fort) found at the east end of the glen provides some evidence of earlier prehistoric habitation.

Abandoned croft in Glen Banchor.

6. Ruthven Barracks, by Kingussie, NN 764 997

Ruthven Barracks near Kingussie were built in 1719 after the first Jacobite uprising of 1715. The smallest and best preserved of the four barracks built during the period, Ruthven Barracks are sited on a large mound surrounded by vast expanses of marshland. They consist of two large stone buildings with enclosing walls. The first stronghold to have occupied this site is thought to date back as early as 1229.

By 1371 it was the home of Alexander Stewart (1343–1405), 1st Earl of Buchan, son of King Robert II of Scotland (1316–1390). After holding the title of Justiciar of Scotia (senior legal officer), he held large territories in the north of Scotland but eventually lost a large part of them. Alexander was formally made Lord of Badenoch in 1371.

Elevation of Ruthven.

ⓘ The mound at Ruthven overlooks an ancient ford and ferry crossing between the barracks and today's Kingussie. This was one of the few crossing places of the middle reaches of the River Spey.

His nickname 'The Wolf of Badenoch' was earned due to his alleged cruelty, but there is no evidence to suggest it was used during his lifetime. Alexander is infamously remembered for destroying Elgin Cathedral further north in 1390, after a dispute with the Bishop of Moray.

The castle at Ruthven was destroyed in 1451 and subsequently re-built on the same mound around 1459 with more advanced fortification.

The surrounding marshlands are said to be some of the most pristine, unspoilt wetlands in the UK. Historically, these areas were drained for farmland and as such very little natural marshland habitat remains.

7. Loch an Eilein Castle, Rothiemurchus Estate, by Aviemore, NH 899 079

Loch an Eilein claims to offer one of the finest views in the Highlands; an island castle with dramatic backdrop of dense forest and high mountain plateau. Loch an Eilein Castle is built on a natural island off the north-west shore and was once said to have been another stronghold of the 'Wolf of Badenoch' (titled Earl of Buchan and also Lord of Badenoch).

The island itself was connected to the shore by an access causeway. However, this has been submerged since the 18th century due to an increase in water level. The castle came into the possession of the Grant family in 1567. Historical records indicate that the Grants were besieged by the Jacobites at the castle during their first rebellion in 1690 on retreat from Cromdale after they lost 400 men in a battle with British royalist forces.

Although lacking the main force of Grant warriors, the people of the loch still managed to hold out in the castle until help arrived. They were led and encouraged by Big Grace (Grizel Mhor) who was said to be the mother of the laird.

Over the years the castle was needed less for defence and safety and as such became unoccupied and derelict. In the late 1800s the castle's damaged walls were skilfully restored and a further maintenance program is now being planned to replace and repair the ancient stonework.

Ducks at Loch an Eilein.

Wildlife along the way

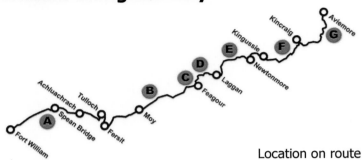

Location on route

A – Glen Spean

This area of Lochaber is the last remaining stronghold for the **Chequered Skipper Butterfly** (Carterocephalus palaemon); it is found nowhere else in the UK. With the name 'Lochaber' literally referring to the area of land between lochs, these water bodies are said to help regulate the temperature, making it favourable for the butterfly. Residing in areas sheltered by woodland, the butterflies feed on the purple moor-grass in the forest meadows.

Also keep a look out in the summer months for **edible wild strawberries** which flank the lower paths through the Leanachan Forest. When passing Spean Bridge you should stay alert for the mainly nocturnal **Scottish Wildcat** (Highland Tiger), as recent local sightings suggest there is still a population in the area.

Leanachan wild strawberries.

ⓘ **Red Squirrel** (Sciurus vulgaris)
As the contours converge eastwards towards Glen Spean, passing through the 8,000 acre Leanachan Forest, keep a lookout for the troubled **Red Squirrel**, whose territories are being pushed continually northwards by its alien rival the **Grey Squirrel**. In 2009 the Forestry Commission identified Leanachan as a strategic stronghold of the Red Squirrel, and an effort is being made across Scotland in conjunction with landowners to preserve this native species. The combined effort will hopefully result in the development of environments that are favoured by Reds but shunned by Greys.

B – Loch Laggan

The centre of Loch Laggan is deep and does not attract much wildlife, so the best places to look are at either end of the loch. Glen Roy to the north is home to the rare and magestic **Golden Eagle**, which can be seen above the loch from time to time. At the dam end, **Red-Breasted Mergansers** and **Goosanders** can often be spotted from the viewpoint. Flocks of **Greylag Geese** are also present in increasing numbers. Scan above the forests at the western end of the loch for **Buzzard**, **Kestrel**, **Sparrowhawk** and the very occasional **Goshawk** displaying in spring.

Look and listen out for the **Green Woodpecker** around this area too, although this is generally considered the edge of its range and one would struggle to find the Green Woodpecker much further north than Newtonmore. The low moorland areas around the loch are home to large herds of **Red Deer** in winter, so called because of their dark reddish brown coat.

C – Strathmashie and the Black Woods

In the rivers and waterfalls of Strathmashie and Pattack, **Grey Wagtails** and **Dippers** can often be seen hopping over boulders and flying close to the water. The woods in this area are home to a vast array of woodland species including **Crossbills**, **Tree Pipet** and **Redstart**. As the woodland fringes make way for open hillside, **Black Grouse** can be found sheltering in the tall grass. Take care, as the Black Grouse is a rare native species and sensitive to human disturbance, especially at its courtship display area, known as the 'lek'.

As well as the **Red**, **Roe** and **Sika deer** population in the area, it is also worth keeping an eye out for one of Scotland's rarer mammals, the **Pine Marten**, which can be very elusive. **Buzzards** can again be seen hunting high above the woods, with **Merlins** and **Kestrels** patrolling the open moorland.

ⓘ Crossbills (Loxia scotica)
The Scottish Crossbill is endemic to the Caledonian Forests of Scotland, and is regarded as the only bird (and vertebrate) unique to the British Isles. The population is thought to be less than 2000 birds. They are specialist feeders on conifer cones, and the unusual bill shape is an adaptation to assist the extraction of the seeds from the cone.

The Scottish Crossbill is extremely difficult to separate from the **Common Crossbill** (depicted here), as plumage distinctions are negligible. The metallic jip call is probably the best indicator, but even this needs to be recorded and analysed on a sonogram to confirm the identity.

D – Spey Dam

Loch Spey is situated between Feagour and Laggan and is in the shadow of the great Pictish fort of Dun da Lamh (see Historical Attractions). A large breeding colony of **Common Gulls** are known to live on the various islands along the River Spey towards Laggan, with the surrounding fields full of **Mountain Hares** in spring. Keep a weather eye out for **Ospreys** which fish close to the dam in summer. You may also see **Red-Breasted Mergansers**, **Common Sandpipers**, **Swifts**, **Tufted Ducks**, **Greylag Geese** and soaring **Buzzards**.

ⓘ **Stoat** (Mustela Erminea)
Watch out for Stoats around Laggan and over open ground. Stoats are carnivores and can hunt prey much larger than themselves, such as rabbits. Its tail has a black tip but can often be white coloured in winter on moorland habitats. The white bobbing tail is often the clearest identification.

E – Around Newtonmore

Newtonmore is known for being prime **Wildcat** country, with an established walking trail and information point bearing the name; keep an eye out for these rare European felines.

The indigenous population has severely declined in Scotland with only around 400 pure wildcats remaining. There are a few thousand more, however, suspected domestic cat hybrids. Keep a lookout for the colourful wildcat sculptures dotted around the town.

Salmon and **Trout** can be seen rising in the river, which in turn attract **Ospreys** and **Otters**. Other birds include the **Buzzard**, **Dipper** and the occasional **Golden Eagle**. **Red Grouse** can be seen on the open moorland as you pass through Glen Banchor from Laggan. The surrounding woodlands are home to **Red Squirrel**, (particularly in the forests passing Cluny Castle) as well as the **Great Spotted Woodpecker**, and occasional **Green Woodpecker**.

F – Insh Marshes RSPB Reserve

The Insh Marshes National Nature Reserve is one of the most important wetlands in Europe. Wetlands such as these have historically been drained to become useful farmland. This pristine wilderness has so far escaped such a fate and as a result provides a unique environment for many species. The area acts as a giant natural sponge, guarding the farmland downstream from floods.

Over 500 species of plants have been identified in this area including small fragrant **orchids**. From the RSPB hides around the marsh, it is possible to see nesting **Lapwing**, **Redshank** and **Curlews**. A flock of one hundred **Whooper Swans** arrive from Iceland each October when the marsh floods. The hides allow long views, so keep a look out for resident **Foxes** and **Roe Deer** over open ground. **Snipe** can be found all year round with the largest numbers in spring. Look out for these waders around the edges of lochans, probing their long beaks into the soft ground.

ⓘ **The Red Fox** (Vulpes vulpes)
Keep a lookout in the evening for Foxes over open ground around the Insh Marshes.

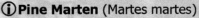
ⓘ **Pine Marten** (Martes martes)
About the size of a domestic cat, Pine Martens have been credited with reducing the population of the invasive Eastern Grey Squirrel in Scotland. Where the range of the expanding Pine Marten population meets that of the Grey Squirrel, the population of the squirrels quickly retreats.

G – Inshriach Forest

Inshriach Forest contains small areas of the most pristine Caledonian Pine Wood still remaining today, and covers a vast area of nearly 3,200 hectares (8,000 acres). Inshriach means 'brindled meadow' or island. These ancient woods are the relics of a once vast forest which covered the UK after the end of the last ice age. Only 1% of this woodland remains today, making it an area of ecological importance, particularly because it harbours some of the country's most endangered species.

Whilst walking through the forest, it is important to keep to the path and keep dogs under close control. Keep a look out for the resident mammals known to occupy these woods; **Red Squirrels**, **Pine Martens**, **Red Deer** and **Badgers**. There are various rare birds on-route: the **Capercaillie**, **Osprey**, **Crested Tit**, **Scottish Crossbill** and **Black Grouse** all make this ancient bog-forest their home. These rare species are sensitive to disturbance, so take utmost care to travel respectfully through their delicate habitat. The forest also shelters a rich pinewood undergrowth of **Blaeberry**, **Cowberry**, **Juniper** and **Heather**. The Heather flowering season is July to September. The purple flowering tops of ling heather have been used to create Heather Ale (Leanne Fraoch) since 2000BC.

Labels on photograph:

Fersit   Inverlair   Tulloch

Moy Reservoir

Moy Bridge

Walking the East Highland Way

- **Section 1** – Fort William to Spean Bridge   11.8 miles
- **Section 2** – Spean Bridge to *Inverlair   9.6 miles
-   2A – Spean Bridge to Achluachrach   6.0 miles
-   2B – Achluachrach to Inverlair (by Tulloch)   3.6 miles
- **Section 3** – Inverlair to Feagour   21 miles
- **Section 4** – Feagour to Laggan   5.0 miles
- **Section 5** – Laggan to Newtonmore   9.1 miles
- **Section 6** – Newtonmore to Kincraig   15.4 miles
- **Section 7** – Kincraig to Aviemore   10.5 miles

(* - Inverlair is close to Tulloch Station Bunkhouse)

Loch Laggan

▶ Section 1
Fort William to Spean Bridge

- **Distance:** 11.8 miles (18.9 km)
- **Terrain summary:** An great start to the route past the Alcan smelter and through the Nevis Range forests. This section offers great views of Ben Nevis. From Torlundy, the way continues north-eastwards through the Leanachan forestry plantation, ascending steadily through Glen Spean. The forest tracks are well established and firm underfoot. Arriving at the Tighnacollie Farm junction the route utilises some great forest trails on the approach to Spean Bridge.
- **Refreshment options:** Fort William, Nevis Range, Spean Bridge.
- **Attractions:** Old Inverlochy Castle, Fort William golf course, Nevis Range with café, bike hire, gondola and mountain bike routes.
- **Accommodation options:** Fort William, Torlundy, Spean Bridge.

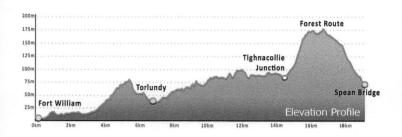

ⓘ Nevis Distillery was established in 1825 and is one of the oldest licensed distilleries in Scotland.

The
BEN NEVIS DISTILLERY
and
Visitor Centre

ⓘ Attraction: Ben Nevis (Beinn Nibheis)
Known simply as *the Ben*, it is the highest mountain in the British Isles and attracts around 100,000 climbers each year. The first recorded ascent of Ben Nevis was made on 17th of August 1771 by the Edinburgh botanist James Robertson, who was in the region to collect botanical specimens.

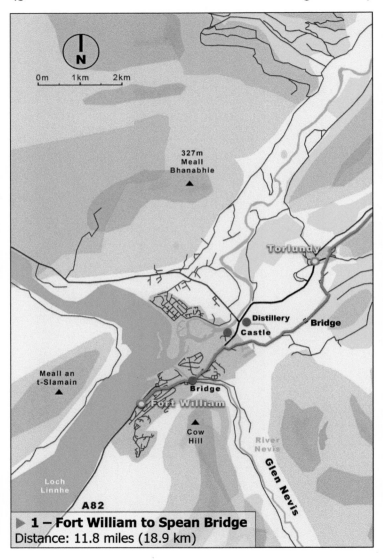

▶ **1 – Fort William to Spean Bridge**
Distance: 11.8 miles (18.9 km)

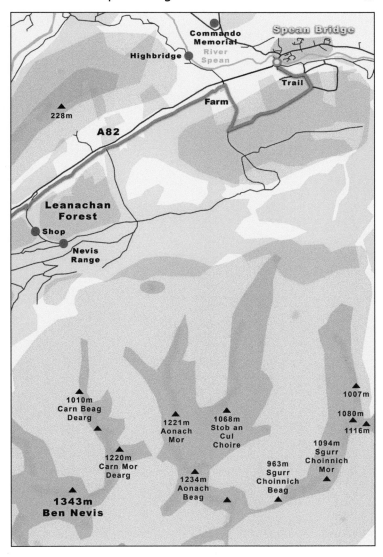

Spean Bridge

Commando
Memorial

Highbridge

River
Spean

Trail

Farm

228m

A82

Leanachan
Forest

Shop

Nevis
Range

1007m

1010m
Carn Beag
Dearg

1080m

1221m
Aonach
Mor

1068m
Stob an
Cul
Choire

1116m

1094m
Sgurr
Choinnich
Mor

1220m
Carn Mor
Dearg

963m
Sgurr
Choinnich
Beag

1234m
Aonach
Beag

1343m
Ben Nevis

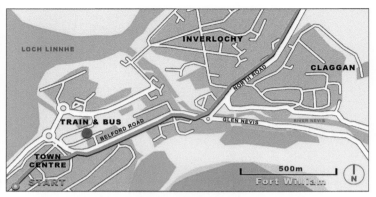

▶   From the new West Highland Way marker at Gordon Square in Fort William town centre, head north-east along High Street, proceeding diagonally through the public green and onto Belford Road. Pass the hospital and swimming pool, turning left over the Nevis Bridge onto North Road.

▶   Turn right, crossing the A82 North Road at the triangular junction signed for the Alcan Smelter (NN 120 750).

ⓘ   In 1929 The British Aluminium Company Ltd completed their major hydro construction programme of dams and vast pipes to carry millions of litres of water to their new aluminium smelters at Fort William and Kinlochleven. Today the Austrialian based company Rio Tinto operates the Alcan aluminium smelter in Fort William.

▶   Cross a railway bridge then turn left just before the level crossing where you then proceed through a double metal gate (NN 121 750). The track leads north-east into a birch wood. Cross a small bridge and follow the track as it curves round to the right bending eastwards. The spectacular hydro pipes on the shoulder of Creag A Chail now come into view up ahead.

▶   It's worth noting that there are many warning signs which urge walkers and cyclists to take care when passing heavy industrial vehicles through this area. Continue along the main track where you pass various Alcan access gates on your right and then proceed straight through a gravel carpark.

▶   Notice the track heads towards some black sheds at the base of the large hydro pipes. The route soon changes in character, leaving behind Fort William's heavy industry. You now enter a forest where the track crosses a cattle grid and proceeds through a gate (NN 130 751).

▶ Continue straight along the track, passing a left turn signed for the 'Public footpath to distillery' (NN 132 751). Very shortly you reach a fork junction as the track winds uphill (NN 133 752). Take the lower track to the left which is aligned with the overhead power cables.

Alcan smelter.

▶ You soon cross a timber footbridge over the Allt Coire an Lochain, where the track becomes more pleasant and cushioned underfoot. The golf course soon becomes visible through the trees to the north.

▶ Cross the spectacular footbridge which spans the high gorge over the Allt A Mhuilinn, taking time to admire the deep pool and waterfall below. You soon pass a timber stile with a path leading off to the right. Continue straight on at this point.

Ben Nevis.

Fort William.

▶ The track becomes a well trodden footpath as it skirts the forest edge south of the golf course. At the next junction turn left downhill, following the sign for the North Face carpark. The track descends steeply past the eastern edge of the golf course at this point (NN 145 761).

▶ At the foot of the hill you arrive at a larger track junction (NN 145 762). Turn left, following signs once again for the North Face carpark. The carpark soon comes into view where you cross a small bridge and pass through a gate – continuing straight on (NN 144 764). The carpark is also known locally as the Allt A Mhulinn carpark.

▶ The track leads northwards for 750 m through the forest plantation, crossing a bridge just before the Torlundy minor road junction (NN 146 771). Turn right along the minor road then immediately left at the Lochaber Forestry sign, passing a large green shed (NN 146 771).

Leanachan Forest.

Forest waymarker.

LOCHABER

▶   At the next junction signposted for the Forestry District Office, turn left leaving the road for a smaller forest track. You are now entering the Leanachan Forest which is famous for both skiing and downhill mountain biking. The Nevis Range gondola is a short walk uphill for skiing enthusiasts with the Snowgoose restaurant and bar available for the non-skiers. For the cyclists, the Witch's Trails in Leanachan were home to the downhill world championships in 2007 with a purpose built 5.2 miles (8.5 km) red route, comprising a total of 270 m of climb and descent. Bikes are available for hire during the summer. Look out for edible wild strawberries which flank the path, ripening from July onwards.

▶   At the next junction, after 100 m, continue straight on through a gate with a white disc identifying the long distance cycle route and a Lochaber waymarker. Notice that you are now following the line of some overhead power cables.

▶   After crossing a small timber footbridge, the way narrows and starts a zig-zag ascent to a larger access road for the Nevis Ski Range (NN 160 783). Turn left and cross the road diagonally, rejoining the forest track some 50 m further downhill. A local farm shop is located 300 m uphill towards the ski range for refreshments.

▶ The next junction (NN 179 796) is clearly marked by an emergency information marker and signage indicating a trail back up to the Nevis Range, 2.1 miles (3.5 km). Take a left at this junction continuing straight on in an easterly direction.

▶ After some ascent, the track soon leaves the forest where you are rewarded with fine views of the surrounding hills; the Ardgour hills to the west and Beinn Bhan (771 m) to the north-west.

ⓘ **Attraction: Nevis Range Mountain Resort**

Sited on the impressive Aonach Mòr, the Nevis Range Mountain Resort offers various activities (weather dependent) which include High Wire Adventure, Ski and Snowboard, Winter Climbing, Forest Walks, Family Cycling, Summer Ceilidh Nights and Downhill Mountain Biking.

For those who would like a view from the summit, you can take the gondola lift and several chairlifts to gain access to the highest station, leaving only a short walk to Aonach Mòr's peak. However, many walkers prefer to avoid the paraphernalia associated with the ski development and approach Aonach Mòr from the south via Glen Nevis, usually climbing both Aonach Mòr and Aonach Beag together. For more info on the resort visit the Nevis Range website at **www.nevisrange.co.uk**.

View of Ben Nevis from the resort.

Leaving the Leanachan Forest for more open ground on the approach to Tighnacoille Farm.

▶ Pass by Tighnacoille Farm and its various outbuildings (NN 208 810), exiting via the main gate. Take care to always leave farm gates as you have found them.

▶ Turn right at the junction past the farm gate, ascending steeply south past the houses at Tom Liath on a narrow tarred track. This section of the route provides great views westward as the track ascends towards the forest plantation.

▶ After a steep climb, you enter the forest and soon encounter a left turn with a gate (noticing a right turn just beyond).

▶ Take the left turn, continuing north-eastwards through the plantation. Notice that the forest track unusually has three distinct furrows and continues on a fairly level grade. Soon you pass a small boggy pond on your left.

ⓘ The **Highbridge** Jacobite memorial is only a short walk from the Tighnacoille Farm junction. Cross the A82 and follow the track for 0.6 miles (1 km) to the cairn and dramatic bridge (see Historical Attractions p19).

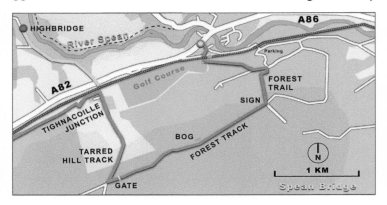

▶ You arrive at a junction signed for the 'circular path', with footpaths leading off to the left and the right. (NN 228 809). Take the footpath left, down through the pine trees until you arrive at a larger track junction also signed for 'circular path'.

Plantation south of Spean Bridge.

Take a left at the sign for Spean Bridge Station, joining the parallel track as it turns north-westwards. Keep right shortly after as the track forks and then narrows, descending through some birch woodland to the station.

You soon arrive at the golf course car park. Cross the railway bridge passing the station building on your right, soon arriving in Spean Bridge by the Commando Bar.

The Spean Bridge circular forest trail.

▶ Section 2
Spean Bridge to Inverlair (by Tulloch)

- **Distance:** 9.6 miles (15.4 km)
- **Terrain summary:** Another easy start to the day by following a delightful forest trail leaving Spean Bridge then a short section of minor road by the River Spean, offering great views of the hills to the south. The route then winds through mature broadleaf forests and open fields approaching Monessie and Achluachrach. This is followed by firmer tracks through the Meall Laire forest plantation dropping steeply to Inverlair. Accommodation can be found at Tulloch, a short walk from the route (1.9 miles).
- **Refreshment options:** Spean Bridge and at Achluachrach (breakfast available at Tulloch Station Lodge Bunkhouse by arrangement).
- **Attractions:** Highbridge Jacobite memorial, by Spean Bridge, Commando Memorial by Spean Bridge, Monessie gorge, Cille Choirille Church by Achluachrach, croft ruins at Achnacochine.
- **Accommodation:** Spean Bridge, (Roy Bridge, 1.8 miles or 3 km from route) Achluachrach, Tulloch.

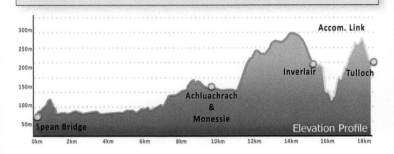

(i) Telford's bridge was built in 1819 and carries the A82 over the River Spean but it is thought the village takes its name from an earlier military-built Highbridge.

In 1913 this earlier bridge, once situated about a mile downstream of the village, collapsed down the deep gorge which it spanned. Local legend tells of the collapse being caused by local school children, who blocked the drainage system the evening before a frost.

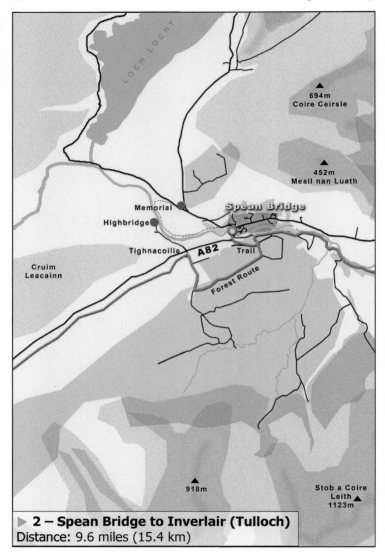

▶ 2 – Spean Bridge to Inverlair (Tulloch)
Distance: 9.6 miles (15.4 km)

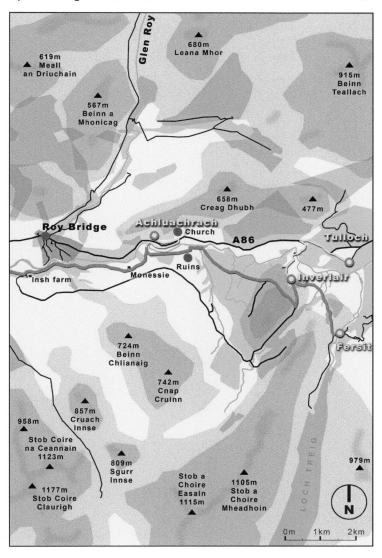

Short history trail

If you have spare time in Spean Bridge it is well worth checking out this great history trail that passes both **Highbridge** and the **Commando Memorial**. To find the start of the trail, follow the A82 for 200 m, turning westwards after the Telford Bridge.

The footpath descends gently to the north bank of the River Spean and then follows the old track bed of a redundant railway line. Shortly after, you arrive at the stunning Highbridge (See historical attractions p21), a derelict military bridge built by General Wade in 1736. The path then turns east, leading to the impressive Commando Memorial. Following the pavement can then take you back to Spean Bridge forming a circular route. The footpath is 2 miles (3.2 km) in length and takes around an hour to walk.

▶ Section 2A
Spean Bridge to Achluachrach
Distance: 6.0 miles (9.7 km)

▶   By the Commando Bar in Spean Bridge, take the station road south, following the single track 100 m to the train station. Cross the bridge and take the forest trail on your left, noticing the timber clubhouse at the Spean Bridge Golf Course high on the right.

▶   Follow the trail again as it ascends through the birch woods passing the right turn avoided previously (p56). At the next junction, take the track left (NN 226 813) leading downhill. The trail twists north then west and finally you arrive at a minor road junction.

▶   Leave the forest trail through a timber gate, arriving at the car park signed for the woodland walk (NN 227 814). Turn right, eastwards towards Killiechonate Lodge (turning left over the railway bridge would take you back to Spean Bridge).

▶   After 400 m, pass a forest track turning on your right and continue straight on (NN 232 815).

▶   At the next junction (NN 238 814) signposted for Corriechoille Lodge, continue left downhill. You quickly leave the forest with farmland opening out on your right which soon offers great views of the hills to the south, Stob Coire Gaibhre (958 m) and Cruach Innse (857 m).

▶   Continue straight on, passing a turning on your right leading south (NN 244 814).

This tarred section runs parallel to the River Spean on your left for the next 1.2 miles (2 km). The route curves south-east towards Insh Farm, crossing a metal bridge over the River Cour (under the bridge is a waist-deep pool good for bathing in summer). Pass a right turn for Killiechonate and a second bridge over the Allt Leachdach.

Turn left at the bridge before Insh Farm driveway (NN 264 802), proceeding through the gate into open farmland past some old agricultural machinery, and then follow the track through the gate, turning right. The route now leads through level fields with grazing cattle and sheep. Pass through some further gates to the east as you enter the broadleaf forests of Coille Innse. The path through the forest appears to be an old drover's road, once paved with stones.

After passing Inshwood (NN 278 805), a small dwelling house nestled in the forest, the track turns uphill through a broadleaf forest over a bridge.

As you leave the trees, dramatic views are presented to the south and east and the remains of a narrow gauge railway can be seen above Monessie, carved some 100 m high on the hillside. Nicknamed the Puggie Line, it was the maintenance railway for the British Aluminium Company's Ben Nevis pipeline, taking water from Loch Laggan and Loch Treig to Fort William to generate the electricity required in reducing aluminium oxide to aluminium metal. The route can be followed today but it is hard work climbing up and down the various gullies. The old railway bridges have decayed over the years making them impassable and dangerous. (On 19th century maps this is still marked as a parallel road skirting the hillside above Monessie.)

Insh Farm.

Old crofter's hut.

Coille Innse forest

ⓘ Attraction: **Glen Spean Viewpoint**

On leaving the forest at Coille Innse you will notice a rusty shelter built high up on the old train line. It's worth walking the steep track up to explore this place and take in the stunning views back down the glen. The old two-room crofter's hut, used only by the local sheep today, looks to have been constructed using the sleepers of the old railway line. In desperate times this could serve as a makeshift bothy, although the sheep dropping carpet would probably put most people off!

View of the route through Glen Spean from the old railway track.

To Monessie

ⓘ Chlinaig Fairies:
You pass an abandoned croft on your right, marked in 1898 OS maps as 'Chlinaig' (meaning 'small declevity or waterfall'), a small settlement named for its proximity to the nearby Chlinaig Falls. It is recalled in Scottish folklore that the last fairies in Lochaber were seen by a man named MacKenzie at Chlinaig. Keep a lookout as you pass by!

▶ You soon enter some woodland through a gate and cross a small bridge (this area can get really muddy). At Monessie Farm (NN 297 805), pass through the tied gate just to the right of the main farmhouse. **When passing through the farm gates (often tied closed) take care to leave them as you found them. The farm also has working dogs so it is advised to keep any pet dogs under close control.** Take the track northwards through the field to the forest edge where a small footpath leads down to a suspension bridge over the stunning Monessie gorge to the left.

▶ After crossing the gorge and railway bridge, turn left at the A86 junction (NN 299 810). Achluachrach offers various accommodation options with refreshments and great food available at the hotel (check seasonal opening times).

Passing Monessie Farm.

ⓘ Attraction: Monessie Gorge
The River Spean suspension bridge.

ⓘ Achluachrach has a great budget hostel with a contrasting luxury hotel with public bar across the road. Visit **www.highland-hostel.co.uk** and **www.glenspeanlodge.com** for further info.

ⓘ **Attraction: Cille Choirill Church, Monessie**

Located high on the dramatic hillside of Bruach Bhristie, overlooking the River Spean, is the picturesque Cille Choirill Church. The Gaelic name 'Cille' means burial ground or church and 'Choirill' refers to St. Cairell, who's monastic cell was historically sited here. With long views east and west over the Braes of Lochaber, this peaceful church may be familiar to some walkers as Glenbogle Church from the BBC's *Monarch of the Glen* TV series. This ancient church is said to have been built by Ailean nan Creach (Allen of the Raids), a 15th century Cameron chief, as a penance for his life of pillaging and violence.

The graveyard is also said to harbour many of the leaders of the last Jacobite uprising of 1745. After a period of extensive renovation, the church officially re-opened in 1932, and remains in good condition today.

Walkers will easily spot the church high on the hillside above Monessie. After crossing the River Spean via the suspension footbridge, cross the A86 and follow the signs from there. This is highly recommended and well worth the steep ascent.

ⓘ **Cille Choirill** has been the ancestral burial place of the MacDonells of Keppoch for centuries. This tall carved stone commemorates Iain Lom MacDonald, a warrior-bard who died in 1709, who is thought to be buried somewhere in the graveyard.

▶ Section 2B
Achluachrach to Inverlair (by Tulloch)
Distance: 3.6 miles (5.9 km)

▶ The way proceeds for the next mile (1.5 km) by following the River Spean eastwards on the south bank. As you re-trace your steps back across the suspension bridge, take the footpath cutting down to the left, following the fence line and the river east through some woodland. (This area is called 'Cnoc an t-Slaoid,' possibly meaning 'round hill of the cart trail'). After entering a gated feild you are presented with glimpse views of the ruins of Achnacochine (NN 309 807) some 10 minutes (0.6 miles or 1 km) walk straight ahead.

▶ Aim for these ruins at Achnacochine, and ultimately the forest plantation beyond. This is easy walking across level ground. Follow the river and tree-line, crossing a deep dry ditch in the field.

Memorial cairns at Cille Choirill.

River Spean at Monessie.

▶   There are various old croft ruins and stone enclosures sited at Achnacochine (originally 'Achinacoshn' meaning 'Field of the Disputants') and it is locally known to have been a once-favoured rendezvous point for cattle reivers while on their travels to Perthshire or Strathspey.

▶   After passing the ruins you approach a gated field, make your way down a slight embankment to your left towards the river passing through some trees. Follow the river east upstream for some 300 m crossing the shallow stony burn of Allt nam Bruach, 'Burn of the Banks'. Note that as you pass the ruins and cross the stream, the path may not be particularly obvious underfoot and the forest gate may appear quite well hidden. Although less intuitive, this is a charming part of the walk which has its own enchanting character.

▶   The stream does become slightly deeper during high rainfall, but is a historical crossing point and maintains a fairly shallow level even in winter. No real boulder hopping required. On 19th century maps, a road can be seen crossing at this point, leading eastwards upstream through what was once native broadleaf forests.

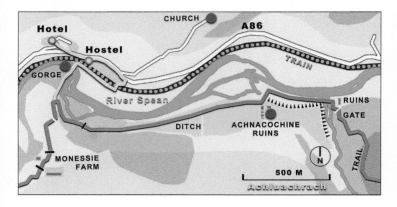

Achnacochine ruins.

Follow the river past Achnacochine.

Achnacochine, meaning 'Field of the Disputants'.

▶   There are some further stone ruins and walls on this east bank of the stream, which hide a timber gate just beyond at the forest plantation edge (NN 314 807). This leads you up a delightful forest trail (not obvious at first) and becomes a larger track further uphill on Coille Chaorainn as you push through the forest.

▶   After 1.2 miles (2 km) of steady ascent, you reach a large mobile phone mast elevated on your right with a series of containers and sheds. Pass with this on your right and ignore the track doubling back also to the right (NN 332 798).

ⓘ The forest gate is located on the east bank of the Allt nam Bruach, beside some further stone ruins.

Fording the Allt nam Bruach just
beyond Achnacochine.

(i) Notice some further hidden croft ruins as you pass through the Inverlair Forest, ascending Coille Chaorainn.

▶ After 0.6 miles (1 km) of curving southeast, you reach a junction where you bear sharply left (NN 339 790), descending steeply to the hamlet of Inverlair (NN 338 798) where the large cream-coloured homestead of Inverlair Lodge comes into view through the trees. This steep hillside is known as 'Tom na Moine' meaning 'the knoll of the peat moss'.

▶ Dating from the late 18th century, the lodge is famous for being one of the places in Northern Scotland where Rudolf Hess, Deputy Leader of Nazi Germany, was held prisoner after his flight to Scotland in May 1941. The Secret Service's goings-on at Inverlair are said to have inspired the 1960s TV series *The Prisoner*.

ⓘ Hitler's deputy imprisoned at Inverlair

The thirteen bedroom Inverlair Lodge was requisitioned by the War Office, much like many large Highland homes during that period. Located a mile west of Tulloch Bunkhouse, it was known as 'Special Workshop No 6' during the Second World War. Special Operations Executive (SOE) agents were thought to be trained there in silent killing, unarmed combat, wireless communications and explosives before being parachuted behind enemy lines. It is also understood to have been a safe haven for secret agents who were at risk.

To this day, it is rumoured that bullet holes can still be seen around the staircase, and a cell-like room inside still has its prisoner observation hatch. In 1941 Hitler's deputy Rudolf Hess flew solo from Augsburg to Scotland in an apparent attempt to negotiate peace with Britain. He was arrested after his aircraft crashed. Local people believe that Hess, the deputy leader of Nazi Germany, was jailed in Inverlair Lodge during the Second World War. The actual reason for his solo flight to Scotland may never be fully understood. Hess died in Spandau Prison, Berlin, in 1987, taking many of his secrets to the grave.

Inverlair Lodge.

▶   At the minor road junction at Inverlair, turn left heading northwards for possible accommodation at Tulloch (meaning 'hill' or 'hillock').

▶   After crossing the River Spean once again the road swings left uphill for 200 m. Turn right at the A86 road junction (NN 341 809) and take the first right after 0.6 miles (1 km) by the red phone box (NN 350 805), following the signs for Tulloch Railway Station for possible accommodation (NN 354 802). (For road walking, follow the guidance outlined in the Highway Code, walking in single file on the right.

ⓘ On 1898 OS maps, Tulloch Station is marked as 'Inverlair Station' with the name Tulloch only referring to a small croft further to the west.

ⓘ Tulloch has a great bunkhouse with self catering cottages at Rushyglen. Visit **www.stationlodge.co.uk** and **www. rushyglencottages.co.uk** for further info.

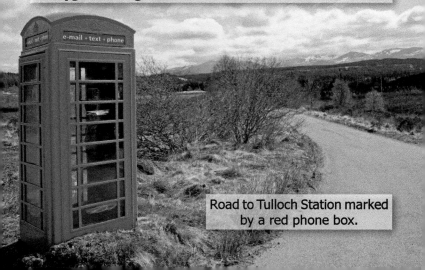

Road to Tulloch Station marked by a red phone box.

Inverlair Falls from the road bridge.

▶ Section 3
Inverlair (by Tulloch) to Feagour

- **Distance:** 21 miles (33.7 km)
- **Terrain summary:** Despite being fairly level and firm underfoot, this is the longest section between accommodation points. The walking is considered easy, utilising hard compacted forest tracks for the most part. The route ascends beyond Fersit, offering glimpses of the Moy Resevoir to the north. From Loch Laggan the route traverses a waymarked estate track through Ardverikie, offering great views of Binnein Shuas to the south and Creag Meagaidh to the north.
- **Refreshment options:** Wolftrax Café, Feagour (open all year), breakfast available at Tulloch Station Lodge Bunkhouse.
- **Attractions:** If you have extra time **Highland Activities** offer a range of outdoor pursuits such as Quad Biking, Paintball and Archery. Visit **www. highlandactivities.co.uk**.
- **Accommodation:** Tulloch, Camping at Feagour. The **Rumblie Guesthouse** in Laggan provides lifts from the Falls of Pattack by prior arrangement (01528 544766). The nearby **Monadhliath Hotel** also offers a pick-up service from Feagour, when possible, via prior arrangement (01528 544276). For a longer stay check out the estate's self catering accommodation at **www.ardverikie.com**.

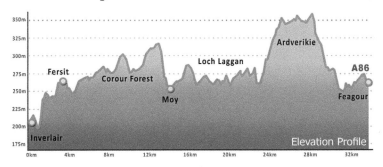

Elevation Profile

Mouth of the River Pattack at the east end of Loch Laggan.

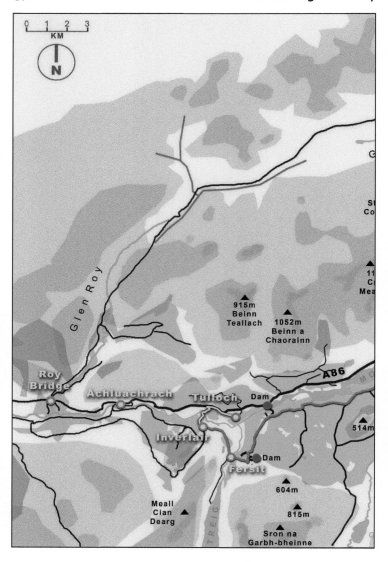

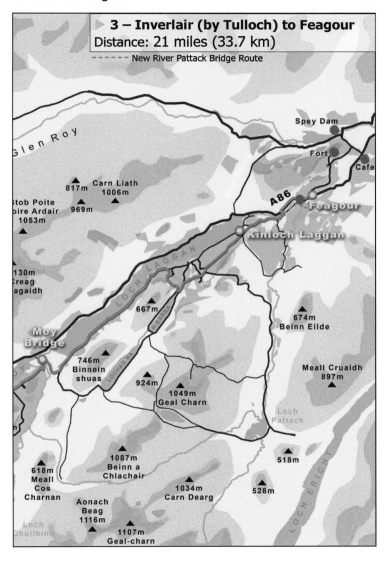

3 – Inverlair (by Tulloch) to Feagour
Distance: 21 miles (33.7 km)
------ New River Pattack Bridge Route

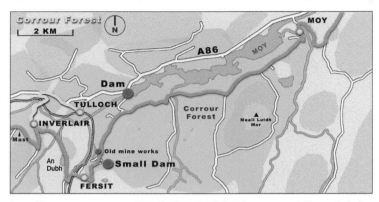

▶   From your accommodation, rejoin the way at Inverlair by doubling-back along the station minor road, continuing west along the A86 for 0.6 miles (1 km) before taking the first left for Inverlair and Fersit.

ⓘ Beside the An Dubh Lochan notice the 500 year old millstone which once belonged to the 2nd Cheif of Keppoch.

▶   Retrace your steps, continuing to Inverlair. Some 200 m past Inverlair Lodge pass a driveway on your left, continue straight for 1.5 miles (2.5 km) to Fersit Bridge, also passing the tranquil An Dubh Lochan (NN 348 788) to the west (meaning 'small black or inky loch').

▶   At the next junction bear left. Cross over the bridge at Fersit over the River Treig, (NN 351 782) ascending past a series of dwellings and farm buildings. As you approach a large agricultural barn at the top of the hill, bear right at the next junction passing with the barn on your left.

ⓘ **An Dubh Lochan** near Fersit. In winter the loch is often frozen with thick ice. View south with the slopes of Stob Coire Sgriodain beyond.

ⓘ An Dubh Lochan between Inverlair and Fersit. There is a good spot for wild-camping at the northern end of the loch. The breeze channelled through the glen from the larger Loch Treig to the south can often keep the midges at bay.

▶ Continue through a gate into open hillside (NN 356 780) with stunning mountain views of Chno Dearg (1046 m) and Stob a Choire Mheadhoin (1105 m) to the south. Follow the track as it swings left entering the Corrour Forest skirting Meall Luidh Mor to the east. (Basically stick to the main forestry track for 6 miles (10 km) between Fersit and Moy bearing eastwards, avoiding the turn-offs to the left and right.)

▶ After 500 m notice small dam workings on your right harbouring a deep pool. Continue straight past another right turn also leading towards the dam. Take a right at the next junction, keeping to the main track (NN 361 787).

▶ Cross a cattle grid and avoid the next left turn northwards which leads downhill into the forest. Instead continue straight on via the main forest track.

Small dam workings near Fersit.

ⓘ Common Frog (Rana temporaria)
Watch out for native frogs on the forest trail. They emerge from hibernation in late February and spawning usually takes place in early March.

Corrour track past Fersit.

Bridge over the Allt Loraich.

▶   The next left turn also curves northwards and leads to the Grade B listed Laggan dam (NN 372 806). The Laggan dam is fenced off to the public for safety reasons so proceed straight on bearing right at this junction, sticking to the main track.

▶   After 1.2 miles (2 km) the track turns north sharply, with a right turn doubling back south. Avoid this and continue straight on along the main track, crossing a small bridge shortly after over the Allt Loraich (NN 388 807).

▶   Continue straight on past the next two large right turns, which both head south, deep into Corrour Forest (NN 407 806 and NN 419 813). Pass a third, smaller right turn which is signed for 'no cars or dogs' leading uphill into the forest. (This leads to open ground just north of Lochan an Tuirc, meaning 'loch of the wild boar').

▶ As you leave the forest you pass a left turn leading towards the Moy Reservoir. The track then turns northwards sharply downhill via a hair-pin bend. Continue straight with Torgulbin Cottage on your left (NN 434 824) and cross the bridge over the Abhainn Ghuilbinn, the descending river outflow from Loch Ghuilbinn to the south.

▶ Turn right at the large junction just beyond Luiblea through a large metal gate (NN 434 828), climbing south for 0.6 miles (1 km) as the track twists uphill, bending east along the river.

View south, the Moy Reservoir drained dry.

▶ Notice the great views of Binnein Shuas (746 m) to the east and take a left at the next junction (NN 443 821) which descends north-eastwards. Fine glimpse views of Loch Laggan are framed to the north. Pass a gate on your right and continue on your descent to the loch shore below. The large expanse of open moorland to your left is often full of deer in vast herds in winter. This area is known as Mointeach Mhor meaning 'great moss-land'.

▶ There are large sandy beaches at both the eastern and western shores of Loch Laggan. Until recently the track skirting the loch was a delightful old mossy forest trail, but has now been replaced with a larger rough forestry track for vehicular access, built using gravel excavated at Moy. This is highlighted by the local council as a 'wider access network' path.

Red Deer at Moy Bridge.

ⓘ Luiblea Cottage, Moy Bridge
This vast expanse of bog is known as Mointeach Mhor meaning 'great moss-land'.

Moy Lodge
There is a huge freshwater sandy beach at the west end of Loch Laggan which is a great spot for wild camping.

▶   Continuing straight, you soon pass the rocky 'Eilean nan Tunnag' on your left, a small island in Loch Laggan meaning 'Island of Ducks'.

▶   After 4 miles (6.7 km) turn right at the next junction following waymarkers as the track begins to ascend (NN 497 870). Notice some Rhododendron bushes uphill at this junction and you can also faintly hear the waterfall in Ardverikie Estate just beyond. At the next junction notice the track splits into 3 (NN 500 867). Bear right, avoiding the central path and the bridge to the left.

▶   The track now ascends steeply with curving switch-backs that hug the contours. You soon cross a babbling brook which is a great place for a water stop

Ardverikie Estate track above Loch Laggan.

▶ As the track descends to the Allt Labhrach (NN 502 859), avoid the track turning downstream and cross the bridge to your left (it's possible at this point to follow the track straight on to visit the weir and Lochan na H-Earba).

▶ On crossing the bridge turn left, following the river downstream (NN 502 859). At the next cross junction bear right as the track begins to ascend (NN 505 863). This track is more recently built and may not appear on older maps.

▶ At the next junction continue straight on (NN 514 866), crossing a small stone bridge over the stream outflow from Loch Doire nan Sgiath (notice that this junction is marked by a large standing stone). It's also worth keeping your eyes peeled for Red Grouse in the tall grass along the forest edge.

▶ Turn left at the next junction (NN 516 868), avoiding the track which leads south. You soon arrive at another junction where you bear right as the track begins to contour the hillside eastwards (NN 516 870). At this cross junction continue straight on noticing a sandy beach and Kinloch Cottage down to your left (NN 535 886).

▶ At the next junction turn right (NN 538 890), soon passing the Ardverikie sawmill (or turn left to explore Loch Laggan's famous beach, said to be the largest inland freshwater beach in Europe).

Laggan Beach.

ⓘ Ice Sculpture.
Loch Laggan's water level is known to fluctuate, which can result in huge shards of winter ice being left beached in beautiful sculptural arrangements.

ⓘ Lochan na h-Earba is situated on the Ardverikie Estate near Loch Laggan and has appeared in the movie Mrs Brown and frequently in the BBC television series Monarch of the Glen.

▶ After passing the modern silver sawmill shed on your left proceed downhill over a cattle grid (NN 541 892).

ⓘ A few kilometres past the sawmill, in the open farmland to the east, is said to be the site of an earlier estate sawmill and water-wheel, a reconstructed replica of which can be found today at the Highland Folk Museum in Newtonmore (see p140).

ⓘ The River Pattack, close to the historical sawmill site.

ⓘ **Replica of the sawmill, Highland Folk Museum.**
The 19th century sawmill, located near Gallovie Farm, had
partially collapsed and was in a state of disrepair. The whole
sawmill was dismantled and relocated to the Highland Folk
Museum in Newtonmore for restoration in 1992. The shed that
had covered the machinery was reconstructed using historic
surveys of the mill.

▶ As you leave the forest for open farmland, a bridge over the river comes into view in the distance. Pass the Gallovie Farm junction (NN 552 894), proceeding left through a traffic barrier approaching the first Pattack Bridge.

▶ The Falls of Pattack are a short road walk upstream from the bridge. To avoid unnecessary road walking, the new route continues straight on from this point along the river, and then passes through the new national park authority gate on the right. Continue over the uneven boggy ground by sticking to the higher tree-line and descend towards the new forestry bridge over the river Pattack. On crossing the bridge, follow the forestry track, turning left at the main junction towards the A86 at Feagour.

▶ Rejoin the way some 500 m past the Fall's car park on the left hand side of the road, entering the forest just before a fenced garden through a metal gate (NN 568 905). This area of Strathmashie is known locally as Feagour (marked as Macoul on 19th century maps).

The River Pattack and the Kinloch Laggan village hall.

Passing Gallovie, approaching Feagour at the A86 junction.

ⓘ Attractions: **Pattack Falls and Wolftrax**

The route passes by an impressive waterfall sited in a steep rocky gorge in the tranquil setting of Feagour beside the A86. There is an interpretation board located at the fall's car park which can give great ideas for short local walks. The pool below the falls is great for swimming in the summer months, although it's worth noting that highland freshwater pools are fairly chilly in all seasons. If time permits, it's well worth exploring the remains of the **deserted village of Druim an Aird** which is located only a short walk from the falls. It's not known why the village was deserted but one theory is that the villagers left after all the men-folk died in a snowstorm while returning from wedding celebrations nearby.

After exploring the area, refreshments are available locally at the **Wolftrax Café**, a short walk eastwards along the A86. Situated in the heart of Strathmashie Forest, the Wolftrax MTB Centre offers a series of challenging downhill routes for novice and experienced mountain bikers alike. If you would like to take some time to give this a try then bike hire is available from the Base Camp station, which also houses a café, toilets, shower and repair centre. For further information and opening times visit **www.basecampmtb.com**.

Author swimming at the falls.

▶   From here you can access accommodation in Laggan by Kingussie taxi (01540 661343) or pick-up service. The Falls are known as a **local wild camping spot** and the pool below the waterfall is great for bathing in the summer months with an eerie dark cave for more adventurous swimmers.

ⓘ **The Scottish Outdoor Access Code suggests:**
Wild camping is low impact, done in small numbers and only for two to three nights in any one place. You can camp in this way wherever access rights apply but avoid causing problems for local people and land managers by not camping in enclosed fields of crops or farm animals and by keeping well away from buildings, roads and historic structures. Take extra care to avoid disturbing deer stalking or grouse shooting. If you wish to camp close to a house or building seek the owners' permission. Leave no trace by:
• Taking away all your litter
• Removing all traces of your tent pitch and any open fires (follow the guidance for lighting fires)
• Not causing any pollution

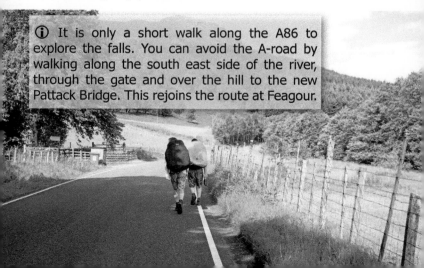

ⓘ It is only a short walk along the A86 to explore the falls. You can avoid the A-road by walking along the south east side of the river, through the gate and over the hill to the new Pattack Bridge. This rejoins the route at Feagour.

The River Pattack.

▶ Section 4
Feagour to Laggan

- **Distance:** 5 miles (8.1 km)
- **Terrain summary:** This is the shortest section of the route, but offers some of the best views as the trail ascends through the Black Woods to an excellent vantage point, just short of the impressive Fort Dun da Lamh. The forest tracks vary in size but are well established and well drained. From the Spey Dam, the route turns eastwards across level farmland, approaching Laggan Village via a quiet tarred road.
- **Refreshment options:** Wolftrax MTB Café, Laggan Village (with shop and bars).
- **Attractions:** Druim an Aird ruins, Fort Dun da Lamh and viewpoint, Falls of Pattack, Wolftrax MTB Centre, Spey Dam at Loch Spey.
- **Accommodation:** Feagour (wild camping only), Laggan has various accommodation options. The **Rumblie Guesthouse** in Laggan provides lifts from the Falls of Pattack via prior arrangement (01528 544766). The nearby **Monadhliath Hotel** also offers a pick-up service from Feagour, when possible, via prior arrangement (01528 544276). The **Kingussie Taxi** service (01540 661343) provides lifts from Feagour to Laggan following the closure of the Glen Cottage B&B - previously sited at the Falls.

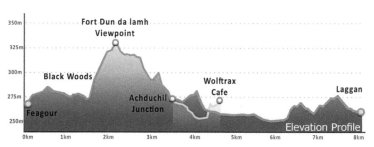

Quiet road approaching Laggan.

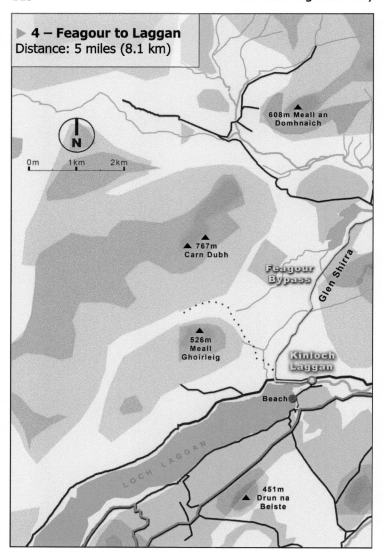

▶ 4 – Feagour to Laggan
Distance: 5 miles (8.1 km)

N

0m   1km   2km

608m Meall an
Domhnaich

767m
▲ Carn Dubh

Feagour
Bypass

Glen Shirra

526m
Meall
Ghoirleig

Kinloch
Laggan

Beach

LOCH LAGGAN

451m
▲ Drun na
Beiste

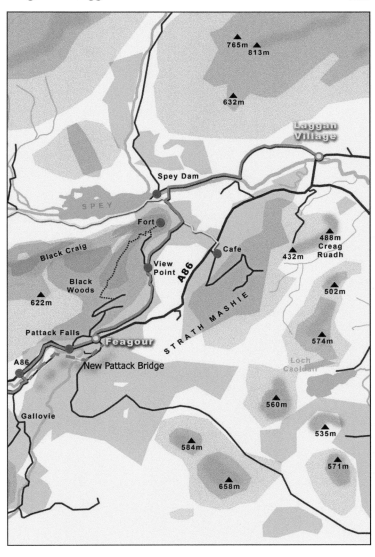

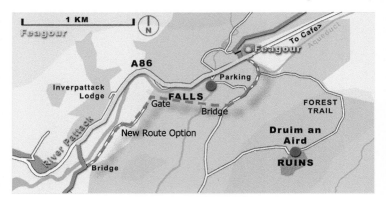

▶   From your accommodation, rejoin the way at the forest junction (NN 568 904), passing through a gate, with a fenced garden on your right. Take the right fork at the junction immediately after, now proceeding on a long level track north-eastwards.

▶   As Strathmashie House comes into view, follow the blue 'Black Woods' waymarker as the forestry track narrows to a footpath and turns uphill through the forest plantation.

▶   You then join a larger forest track at the top of the trail (NN 579 917). Turn right and enjoy the fine views over Laggan from the picnic bench. From this viewpoint, you can take a side trip to the hill-top fort Dun da Lamh (NN 582 929), an ancient Pictish settlement (see Historical Attractions p25).

▶   From this junction, the way descends to the right, following signs for Achduchil and enters the lower forest plantation.

▶   As you approach a timber gate and stile, notice the blue 'Black Woods' waymarker once again.

The western summit of Black Craig (622 m) above Inverpattack.

The trails through the Black Woods are waymarked and well sign-posted between Feagour and the Spey Dam.

Blackwoods Walk

Scotland Map

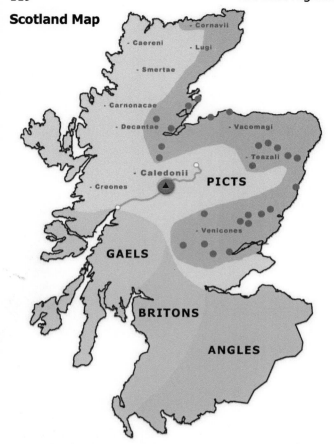

Territorial boundaries around AD 800.

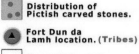

Distribution of
Pictish carved stones.

Fort Dun da
Lamh location. (Tribes)

East Highland Way.

① After their time in Scotland, the Romans made references to a powerful Caledonian tribe (Caledonii) residing in the north. This corresponds with later Pictish history as having been a main centre of power for the Picts.

ⓘ **Plan of Fort Dun da Lamh**

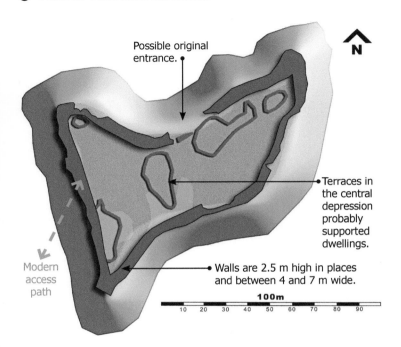

Possible original entrance.

N

Terraces in the central depression probably supported dwellings.

Modern access path

Walls are 2.5 m high in places and between 4 and 7 m wide.

100m

10 20 30 40 50 60 70 80 90

ⓘ Attraction: **A strategic stronghold**

Fort Dun da Lamh was skilfully erected during the earliest Pictish period using 5000 tons of stone. Strategically, the fort was constructed 600 ft high on the impregnable Black Craig with its defensive walls 7 m thick in places. It is thought that this rocky eminence represented a frontier fortress, guarding the Pictish farmland to the north and east. From here, it would have been easy to spot marauding invaders advance from the south and west, making this location perfect for a defensive stronghold (see Historical Attractions p25).

Spey Reservoir from Dun da Lamh.

Remains of Fort Dun da Lamh's defensive walls on the eastern summit of Black Craig.

Dun da Lamh from the Spey Dam.

▶   At the next junction (NN 586 930) take a right for some refreshments at the Wolftrax Café (downhill mountain bike centre NN 593 923, see attractions on p115) or turn left to continue the way towards the Spey Dam.

▶   After 800 m turn right onto the tarred road (NN 583 934) crossing the bridge over the River Spey. The way continues right after the bridge or turn left to explore the Spey Dam. Laggan now comes into view across the fields to the east.

▶   You arrive in Laggan village (Laggan, meaning 'little hollow') approaching the A86 junction, with the Laggan Stores, toilets, post office and picnic area (NN 615 943). Laggan village has various accommodation and refreshment options.

Laggan from the viewpoint below Dun da Lamh.

The Spey Reservoir.

▶ Section 5
Laggan to Newtonmore

- **Distance:** 9.1 miles (14.6 km)
- **Terrain summary:** The route passes through Laggan village as far as Balgowan along the A86 (highlighted as a future core path by the Cairngorm National Park Authority). From here the path crosses the open moorland of Strath an Eilich where you eventually join the larger Cluny Estate track. Following the river beyond Dalnashallag Bothy, the track becomes slightly boggy and less obvious in places. Finally you reach a firmer track at the east end of Glen Banchor, which descends gently towards Newtonmore, passing a splendid viewpoint with benches.
- **Refreshment options:** Laggan, Newtonmore.
- **Attractions:** Climb any of the surrounding Munros, explore the ruins and historical settlements of Glen Banchor, walk the Newtonmore Wildcat Trail or explore the Highland Folk Museum.
- **Accommodation options:** Laggan, Newtonmore. (There is a bunkhouse in Laggan and two hostels in Newtonmore, with Dalnashallag Bothy halfway between in Glen Banchor.)

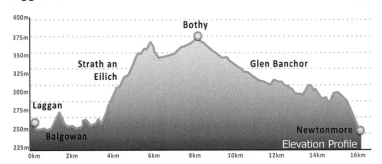

The route through Strath an Eilich.

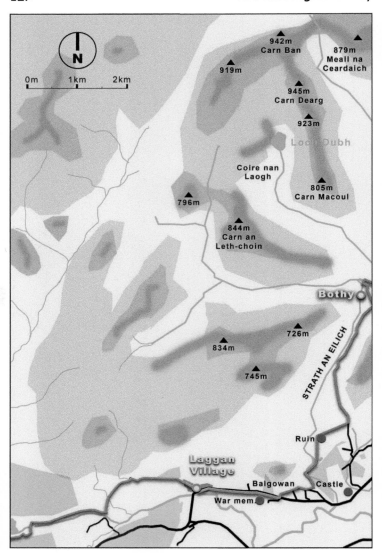

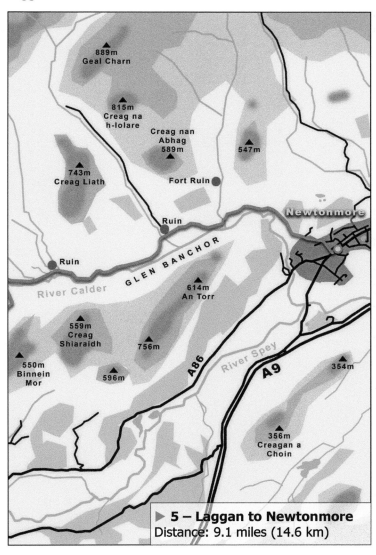

▲ 889m
Geal Charn

▲ 815m
Creag na
h-Iolare

Creag nan
Abhag
589m ▲

▲ 547m

▲ 743m
Creag Liath

Fort Ruin ●

Ruin ●

● Ruin

GLEN BANCHOR

River Calder

▲ 614m
An Torr

559m ▲
Creag
Shiaraidh

▲ 756m

A86

River Spey

A9

▲ 550m
Binnein
Mor

▲ 596m

▲ 354m

356m ▲
Creagan a
Choin

Newtonmore

▶ **5 – Laggan to Newtonmore**
Distance: 9.1 miles (14.6 km)

▶ From Laggan Stores proceed along the A86 for only 1 mile (1.6 km) until you reach the Balgowan township just beyond the Laggan Country Hotel. Take a left uphill at the single-track road signed for Balgowan (NN 631 941).

▶ After around 660 m you arrive at the top of the Balgowan road crescent. Notice a large double metal gate to your left (NN 637943). Continue down the road for a further 120 m, passing some semi-detached cottages on your left.

▶ Just after these cottages turn sharply left and ascend a steep gravel footpath below some large conifer trees. As the path curves north-east, bypass the cottage by taking the small, faint trail on your left (some 20 m before the garden gate).

▶ Follow this footpath until the deer fence turns left. At this point continue along the trail as it shadows the inside of the deer fence. You soon pass through a kissing-gate where you then turn instantly right through another stock gate, now on a good track.

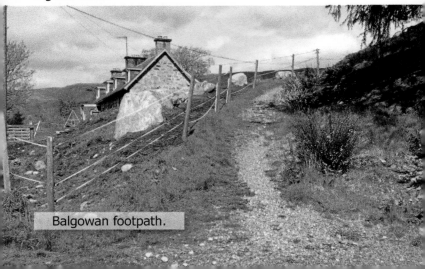

Balgowan footpath.

Lagbuidhe
ruin gate

Fence line past Balgowan.

▶ Cross the first stream immediately to your right (NN 636 947). Ford the 2nd shallow burn and rejoin the larger track again only for a short time. From this point you are on open moorland and the general aim is the join the obvious Cluny Estate track which can be seen cutting across the foot of Binnein Beag to the north-east.

ⓘ Livestock graze in this area so please keep gates closed.

▶ As the track fords the second larger stream do not cross. Instead, turn right at this point around a swollen river bend and follow the burn upstream – shadowing the fence-line on your right. Aim towards two wind-beaten trees and some stone ruins upstream which mark the ruined croft of Lagbuidhe (NN 637 952).

ⓘ Lagbuidhe croft was said to have been abandoned around 1870. Kept by a widower, with but one daughter, who in spite of all his care, caught a slight touch of the pregnancy, but wouldn't reveal who she'd caught it from. The shame was too much for her father, so, without revealing his 'difficulty' to the rest of Balgowan, he sold all his stock, and early one morning stole away over the hill to Newtonmore, the railway, and Australia, where it is said he did very well indeed!

The Cluny Estate track through Strath an Eilich.

▶ Pass through a rusty-brown gate at the north-west corner of the ruins (NN 637 953) and immediately join a faint evolved path where it breaks the wall line of the enclosure. Follow this left across open ground, bearing in the general direction of the prominent hill; Binnein Beag to the north-east.

▶ Although fairly faint in places, this is a delightful trail over well drained moorland. You soon encounter an older ruined steading around NN 642 957. Just beyond this the path joins the Cluny Estate track where you continue left (northwards) through Strath an Eilich to Glen Banchor. (NN 644 959)

▶ After passing the stalker's bothy at Dalnashallag (NN 648 984), also known locally as Carnegie's Bothy, cross the stream by the shallows directly to the right. This may involve some boulder-hopping and can become deep during wetter weather (see alternative route if streams are impassable p137).

▶ Follow the River Calder eastwards downstream as it carves its way through the glen, finally descending towards Newtonmore. The path becomes increasingly less obvious in places but is still a fairly easy and level walk.

Stalkers at Dalnashallag.

ⓘ Across the stream just north of the stalker's bothy at Dail na Seilg (meaning 'meadow of the hunting'), in previously cultivated land lies the ruins of a depopulated township, evicted in the mid-19th century during the highland clearances. Today, the remains of the township comprise of the footings of 18 buildings (and kiln), all varying in size with larger sheep pens sited further to the north.

Walking west through Glen Banchor.

Boulder-hopping at Dalballoch.

▶   The only real obstacle in the glen is a shallow boulder crossing where various water courses converge just south of the Dalballoch ruins (Dail Ballach – 'meadow of the mottled place', NN 659 986).

ⓘ   Dail Ballach is another old farmstead deserted during the clearances. Situated between the Allt an Lochain Dubh and the Allt Ballach, the township once comprised of six buildings and two enclosures. The metre-wide stone footings can still be seen today just north of the ruined croft.

▶   Cross the streams close to the main river. These streams are fairly shallow and split into four small sections but do require a few challenging boulder-hops. This is fairly easy to negotiate in both summer and winter and provides a fun navigational challenge for the less agile.

▶   Soon after, veer towards a timber gate which comes into view beyond some boggy ground. Notice the erosion of the river banks to your right which has exposed both sandy and peaty sub-soils over time as the land has been reshaped by the passing watercourse. Look out for Grouse in this area hiding amongst the tall grass along the rivers edge.

▶   You pass a ruined croft on your right, another remnant of the clearances, with the larger depopulated township of Dail an Tullaich across the river to the south. This can be seen marked on OS maps to this day although it is not visibly obvious from the path.

▶   Notice a deer fence and timber gate ahead, some 250 m eastwards. Pass through the gate, entering the forest. After 100 m you cross a small shallow stream, notice the stone ruin on your right with large abandoned crofts up on your left (NN 679 991).

Dalballoch ruin.

▶   Arriving at Glenballoch (which until recently was the last inhabited house in the glen, NN 679 993), you arrive at the start of a larger track which is much firmer underfoot. Stepping over a small stile, turn right as the track leads eastwards crossing a bridge after 30 m.

▶   Pass through a wooden gate and cross a small timber bridge known as Dalchurn Bridge, also locally called the Shepherd's Bridge (NN 692 997, Dalchurn – Dail a' Chaorainn, meaning 'the meadow of the rowan tree'). You soon arrive at the Glen Road car park leading to Newtonmore.

▶   Soon after, pass some welcome benches with charming views south over the River Calder. There are good footpaths down to the river and the Newtonmore Wildcat trails are close by. As this is prime wildcat country it is worth keeping an eye out for these rare European felines. (The wildcat footpath leads down-stream to Newtonmore should you wish to explore this slightly longer route.)

ⓘ As the Glen Road starts descending towards Newtonmore, (literally meaning 'new town on the moor') you pass an old well marked 'Well of the Alder' which is a natural water spring used by the locals for generations. The well is brick-built and thought to be Victorian. The original Gaelic name for the spring, 'Fuaran lag an Dromain', means 'the well of the hollow on the ridge'.

▶   You soon arrive at a fork junction (NN 711 992). Take the smaller tarred path marked by a line of streetlights down to your right towards the town. This is known as the 'Old Glen Road'. After a few hundred metres you arrive in Newtonmore Main Street with various accommodation and refreshment options.

ⓘ   For an alternative route follow the signposted 'Wildcat Trail' south from the viewpoint – following the River Calder on well established paths, soon arriving at the west end of Newtonmore town centre.

ⓘ Laggan to Newtonmore alternative
via Glentruim 9.6 miles (15.5 km)
(Further info on OS Map Explorer 402 or Landranger 35)

▶   This route involves a reasonable amount of walking on quiet country roads and cycle tracks. However, it is a picturesque alternative when the Glen Banchor route is impassable due to the River Calder being in spate (flood). From Laggan Stores (NN 614 943) turn right and cross the bridge over the River Spey and continue along the A86 Trunk Road. After 650 metres you will reach a road junction on your left (NN 613 937).

▶   Turn left onto this road (A889) signposted Dalwhinnie/ Perth. Follow the road uphill for 1.45 miles (2.3 km) and you will reach a junction on your left signposted Glentruim. Turn left onto this quiet country road. After a while the road starts to climb gently uphill and after 3 miles (4.8 km) you reach a large memorial cairn to Clan MacPherson (NN 677 941). The cairn is dedicated to Ewan MacPherson of Cluny (1706 - 1764), a Jacobite and veteran of the 1745 rebellion. From here you have a great view of the River Spey as it meanders to its source.

▶   From the memorial continue east and uphill for 80 metres until you reach an opening for Truim Woods on your right (NN 678 942), signposted for 'Paths Around Laggan'. Turn right into the woods and continue along the broad forest track, do not take tracks to your right or left. After 325 metres (NN 678 938) you then turn left onto another forest track.

▶   This track winds its way past overhead electricity pylons before swinging left and north. At the next junction (NN 685 943) go straight on in a north-westerly direction. After 1 mile (1.6 km) you will rejoin the minor country road.

▶   Turn right onto this road and as you wind along it you will pass a caravan park on your left just before crossing the River Truim (NN 689 949).

▶   From Bridge of Truim continue uphill on the minor road and after 400 m you cross a railway bridge. At this point (NN 691 951) you will see the busy A9 trunk road ahead of you and National Cycle Route No. 7 to your right and left. Turn left onto the cycle path which runs parallel to the A9. Continue on the cycle path (ignoring any turns to the left or right) and the route now follows the narrow old A9 road to Inverness. After 0.9 miles (1.45 km) the old A9 joins a minor road (NN 696 965), take care at this point as the road can be busy with cars for the nearby Ralia Café.

▶   After 0.6 miles (1 km) you reach a junction (you will have passed the Ralia Café on the way). The busy A9 Trunk Road is on your right, however, you turn left onto the B9150 signposted for Newtonmore and various visitor attractions (NN 704 970). Walking along the verge of this road you will cross the main railway line north to Inverness and then the River Spey again. As you approach Newtonmore you will be walking on pavement and after 1.5 miles (2.4 km) you will be in the middle of Newtonmore at the Wildcat Centre and Town Hall (NN 714 990).

MacPherson Memorial, Glentruim.

ⓘ Attraction: **Loch Imrich, Newtonmore**

Just behind Newtonmore's Main Street is the tranquil Loch Imrich, a delightful side trip if you can spare the time. The loch is known geologically as a 'kettle hole' (toll-coire), meaning that it is an enclosed pond with no outlet stream. It is thought that the loch was formed when a receding glacier left behind a giant block of ice which became isolated in the soft ground. When the heavy block melted, it left a deep depression in the soft sand and gravel deposits below. There are apparently other such 'kettle holes' around Newtonmore.

Loch Imrich.

Highland Folk Museum, traditional dwelling.

ⓘ Attraction: **The Highland Folk Museum**

The award winning Highland Folk Museum is a one-mile-long living history site which can be found at the east end of Newtonmore. The museum opened in 1995 and utilises its farmland, woodlands and open area to showcase the domestic and working conditions of the Highland people from the 1700s to the present day. With re-enactments, working demonstrations and lots of authentic buildings, this lively attraction can take a good few hours to look around so plan your day carefully to explore it in full. Visitors to the site can also take advantage of the café facilities, toilets, play park and picnic area. Visit **www.highlandfolk.com** for opening times and information about the attractions on offer (it is worth remembering that the museum is closed during the winter months).

▶ Section 6
Newtonmore to Kincraig

- **Distance:** 15.4 miles (24.7 km)
- **Terrain summary:** Departing Newtonmore, the route continues east before taking the Wildcat Trail north and the waymarked Loch Gynack track east to Kingussie. From Ruthven, the route connects with the established and well marked Badenoch Way. This stretch of the journey connects a varied range of paths through open moorland and mature broadleaf forests. After passing by sleepy hamlets and descending through forestry plantation, the route arrives at the shores of Loch Insh, a short walk from Kincraig.
- **Refreshment options:** Newtonmore, Kingussie, Insh Watersports Centre, Kincraig.
- **Attractions:** The Highland Folk Museum, Clan Macpherson Museum, Ruthven Barracks, RSPB bird hides, Insh Watersports Centre.
- **Accommodation options:** Various around Newtonmore, Kingussie, Loch Insh and Kincraig.

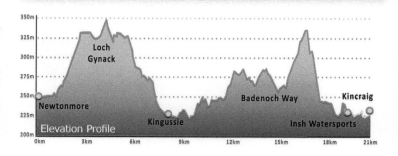

Ruthven Barracks, with the Cairngorm foothills beyond (see Historical Attractions p27).

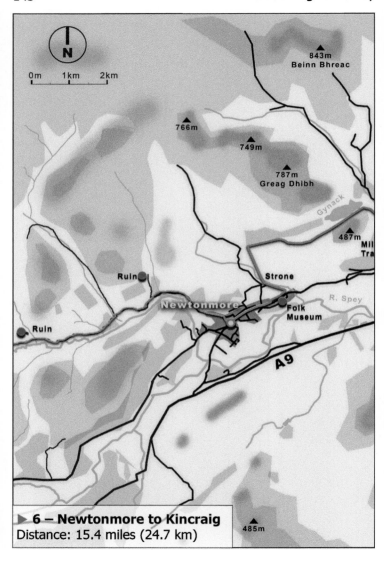

▶ 6 – Newtonmore to Kincraig
Distance: 15.4 miles (24.7 km)

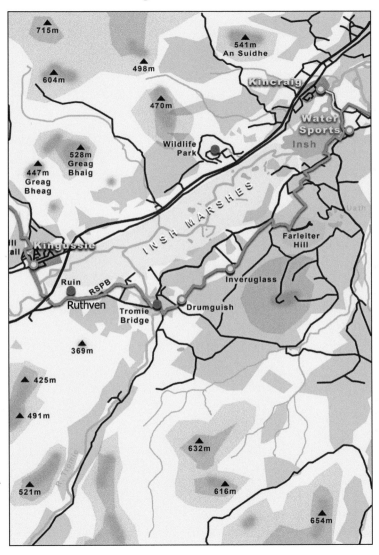

▶   From your accommodation, rejoin Newtonmore Main Street, continuing eastwards towards Kingussie. Past the gated entrance to Ard-na-Coillie House opposite the Highland Folk Museum (NN 726 996), the pavement transforms into the Newtonmore Wildcat Trail. Follow this narrow footpath as it winds through woodland shadowing the A86.

▶   As you climb steps and pass through a stile the footpath becomes less distinct. After passing through a second stile you arrive at a small carpark where you rejoin the footpath at its far side (NN 728 998).

▶   As you pass through another stile the Allt Laraidh now comes into view. Head upstream and through a gate as the path twists uphill through woods. A dramatic waterfall soon comes into view where you pass over a stile and cross a footbridge (NH 725 001). This area may contain livestock so dogs should be kept under close control.

▶   From the footbridge the route is not obvious. Stick to the waterfall stream and join a narrow trail on the hillock above (NH 723 002) which leads to a metal stile (notice a wildcat waymarker). If you find yourself at a second footbridge beside Strone croft, retrace your steps back to the waterfall and rejoin the path which is just out of view above the falls.

▶   Pass through the stile onto open hillside noticing some great wild camping spots just up ahead on your right. The track at this point is less distinct so head northwards in the direction of the forestry plantation straight ahead. Rejoin the track just to the right of the large stone sheep enclosures (NH 721 004) known locally as Strone fank (Strone meaning 'headland' and fank meaning 'sheep fold').

▶ After you pass the walled sheep enclosures cross the timber footbridge on the right. Notice the track now ascends along the right hand bank of the stream (NH 720 006). The path becomes an evolved sheep trail as it approaches the forest edge.

▶ Head for the gate at the forest corner where you pass through a sculptured break in the stone wall (NH 719 012). Follow the track eastwards along the forest edge noticing waymarkers signed for Kingussie.

▶ Cross a timber footbridge and follow the path onto open moorland as it leads away from the forest line (NH 726 014). Loch Gynack soon comes into view on your left (this is another spot where you should keep your eyes peeled for Red Grouse darting through the heather). At the next path junction follow the Kingussie waymarker right. Notice that the path now bends south for a brief period then soon heads back towards the loch.

The waymarked trail to Kingussie.

▶   After passing through a gate in the stone wall (NH 733 013) notice the path now aims for some higher ground to the south of Loch Gynack. Notice also the waymarker at the top of the next rise. The track narrows as it cuts through the heather and Pitmain Estate soon becomes visible at the east end of the Loch.

▶   The path contours pleasantly along the loch shore and soon cuts through a mossy boulder field. At the next junction follow the golf course circular sign straight on (NH 748 023), leading south away from the loch (avoid the left turn down to the gate and the right which heads up Creag Bheag).

A burn near Strone.

Loch Gynack.

▶   As the footpath becomes smaller you soon encounter another golf course waymarker and cross some boards over boggy ground. You are soon presented with views of Kingussie golf course to the south. The narrow footpath descends through woodland arriving at a picturesque bench and viewpoint.

▶   Gaiters are advised through this area as the evolved footpath can become very boggy in wet conditions. Pass through a stone wall and a gate following the signpost for Kingussie. As you follow some overhead power lines (NH 752 018) the golf course soon appears on your left. At the next junction turn left through the gate and head down the stony track of the caravan park (NH 754 014). Turn right at the tarred Gynack road for Kingussie.

ⓘ Attraction: **The Gynack Mill Trail**

▶ From the interpretation board and sign you can follow the delightful Mill Trail down the Gynack burn to Kingussie.

▶ The Gynack burn has provided sustainable power to the people of the area since the late 1700s. It was used to drive wool and flax mills but today supplies power via a hydro-electric scheme.

▶ As you turn left and cross the Gynack footbridge, look out for the native Red Squirrel in the surrounding woodland especially early in the morning.

▶ At the next road junction turn right following the sign for the Gynack Mill Trail.

▶ After around 60 m the path cuts between some gardens on the right and leads back to the river. The trail twists through a wood of birch and hazel and you soon pass a deep gorge.

ⓘ It's worth keeping your eyes peeled through this area for the Rannoch Sprawler, a rare moth found only in the Highlands.

▶ At the next junction turn right towards the river and continue to follow the waymarkers. You soon pass the lade interpretation board and viewing gallery.

▶ Turn right and cross the final footbridge where you rejoin the Gynack road once again. Turn left and continue towards Kingussie, now only a few hundred metres downhill.

ℹ️ **The Rannoch Sprawler Moth**
This rare moth favours a habitat of ancient birch (Betula) woodland, where it is possible to locate the adults on the tree trunks during the day. The normal flight time is at night when it will come to light.

▶ Opposite the Duke of Gordon Hotel, turn right down a minor road (NH 756 006), following signs for Ruthven Barracks, soon passing a war memorial garden on your left (Ruthven – from the Gaelic, 'Ruadhainn', meaning 'upland fortress' or 'heap').

▶ Continue straight passing the Silverfjord Hotel on your left and train station on your right. (Take care passing over the level crossing; see the Highway Code for advice.)

▶ Join the footpath on the left, parallel to a small river (a tributary of the River Spey), passing some shinty pitches on your right. Shinty is unique to Scotland and is said to be one of the oldest games in the world, a team game similar to hockey but more violent!

▶ As you approach a small picnic area, notice the river bending eastwards below to join the larger Spey. Pass through a stile and continue left along the minor road, crossing a bridge. This trail to Ruthven is known as the 'Jubilee Walk'.

Kingussie.

ⓘ Attraction: **The Highland Wildlife Park**

The Highland Wildlife Park is slightly off-route as it's situated between Kingussie and Kincraig on the north side of the busy A9. Scottish Citylink offer a limited bus service or alternatively just hop into a Kingussie Taxi for the fairly short journey to the park. Created in 1972, the park is open every day of the year (weather permitting) and is host to a number of exciting attractions and creatures including Polar Bear, Wolf, European Elk, European Bison, Bactrian Camel, European Forest Reindeer, Domesticated Yak, Himalayan Tahr and the Kiang or Tibetan Wild Ass.

The park was once home to several examples of the famous black 'Kellas Cat' and other local felines, including a Puma that was reputedly captured locally by a farmer. For info and opening times visit **www.highlandwildlifepark.org**.

Scottish Wildcat at the Wildlife Park.

▶ Pass a sign for the Badenoch Way. (This is a waymarked path that makes up this leg of the route through Insh Marshes.) Pass yet another sports pitch on your right, cross a large bridge over the Spey and continue under the A9 flyover.

▶ At the next junction turn left – following the signs for Ruthven and the Badenoch Way.

▶ Pass Ruthven Barracks (NN 764 997) and continue for 0.6 miles (1 km) along the B970. After a short ascent you soon arrive at the car park for the Insh Marshes RSPB reserve (NN 775 999). This marks the start of the Badenoch Way.

▶ Follow the white markers for the Invertromie Trail. Head up the ramped path to the right, noticing the new timber RSPB bird hide. Continue through a gate at the end of a stone wall on the left.

▶ Cross a bridge following the Invertromie Trail and pass a sign for another bird hide which is located further down the hill.

▶ Follow the white markers through more open ground with great views across the Insh Marshes to the north. Marshland habitats have historically been drained for more useful farmland, making Insh one of the last remaining examples of a large unaltered marshland in Scotland.

▶ At the next gate and junction, follow the waymarker to the right or visit the picnic area and viewpoint 100 m further to your left.

▶ At the next gate, you cross over a larger track and pass through a second gate opposite.

Follow way-markers for the 'Badenoch Way' beyond Ruthven Barracks.

ⓘ **Attraction: Invertromie bird hide**. The new hide offers great views across the marshes with useful wildlife interpretation boards.

▶ Continue straight as the trail ascends through some woodland where you soon arrive at a viewpoint and bench overlooking the River Tromie. Pass through another gate.

▶ Pass a sign for the 'old church yard' to your left and descend through the woods to a track running parallel with a stone wall following it right. After passing another gate, the path continues through a narrow gap between a stone wall and tree. As the path leads through the forest towards the River Tromie, pass through a stile and more open ground with a backdrop of pines across the river.

▶ At the minor road junction, pass through the gate and turn left over the old stone Tromie Bridge (NN 789 995) with splendid views of the tumbling river (see below).

▶ After crossing the bridge, turn right onto a good forest track. After a further 300 m, turn sharply left at the next junction following signs for the Badenoch Way (NN 790 992), as the track ascends between some old stone walls.

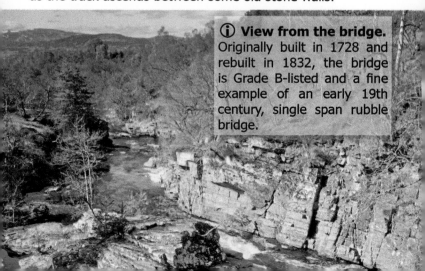

ⓘ **View from the bridge.** Originally built in 1728 and rebuilt in 1832, the bridge is Grade B-listed and a fine example of an early 19th century, single span rubble bridge.

Insh Marshes.

▶ You soon arrive at the small hamlet of Drumguish (NN 794 995), and continue straight – passing a post box on your left. (Avoid the turn right, signposted for a right-of-way.) Continue straight, leaving the tarred lane and entering a forest plantation through a gate.

▶ Cross some boggy ground using the timber duck boards then pass through a timber gate marked for the Badenoch Way. As you leave the forest and cross the stream, the route passes some large overhead power lines.

▶ As you head north-east flanked by heather, this part of the trail offers glimpse views of the Cairngorm Mountains to the east (Cairngorm meaning 'greeny-blue hill') and the Insh Marshes to the north.

▶ At the small hamlet of Inveruglass, the route joins a larger track proceeding through a gate.

▶ As you leave Inveruglass the access road bends right. Continue left at this junction through a gate proceeding straight ahead for a short time. Continue straight at the next junction following the sign for Insh and pass a picnic bench surrounded by Juniper bushes. Pass through a second gate.

▶   At the next junction with the house and driveway, turn right through a green metal gate. After a second green gate, turn left at the next junction ascending into the forest via a large forestry track. After a few hundred metres turn left onto the smaller waymarked footpath entering the forest.

▶   Crossing the duck boards over more boggy ground, you soon join a larger track turning left. The track continues downhill, where you turn right at the bottom junction.

▶   After a few hundred metres, the route breaks off from the main track, turning left at the waymarker, following the path downhill. Turn left at the bottom junction, descending steadily as the track swings northwards towards the minor road at Balncraig (NH 827 033).

▶   As you pass through the gate at the foot of the hill, turn sharply right just before the minor road, following a small path that runs parallel, soon crossing a burn.

▶   At the next minor road junction, cross the road diagonally through the waymarked gate.

▶   Follow the waymarkers through the forest trails as the route leads downhill towards Loch Insh.

▶   At the shore viewpoint over Loch Insh, the route turns right, uphill via some timber steps, along a short ridge and descends via more timber steps.

▶   As you rejoin the minor road turn left. Notice the waymarker at Inshbrec and turn left again passing between some garden gates. You soon pass a play area and some boating practice pools at the Loch Insh Watersports Centre.

ⓘ Attraction: **Loch Insh Watersports Centre**

The route passes by Loch Insh which has become renowned in recent years for its great watersports and activity centre. If further physical exertion seems like too much after a hard day's walk, it's always worth stopping here for some dinner or a drink at the bar. Activity highlights include sail sports, paddle sports, raft building and pedalos. For the visitors who prefer sticking to dry land, the centre has various activities on offer including a dry ski slope, archery and kids' play park, not to mention woodland walks and mountain bike trails. The Boathouse Restaurant has great views over the Loch, where you can usually sit in comfort and watch wind-surfers of all abilities inevitably falling into the loch! For those who wish a longer stay, they have 24 ensuite rooms, including single, twin, double and family. For a full list of the activities on offer it's worth checking **www.lochinsh.com**.

Watersports Centre.

Loch Insh from Kincraig.

▶   After passing the artificial ski slope, you arrive at a small sandy beach (NH 837 045), with impressive views over Loch Insh. From here you can find plenty of accommodation and amenities at Kincraig (meaning 'at the head of the crag') by continuing to follow the Badenoch Way around the loch. Other accommodation can also be found near the activity centre or Feshiebridge.

▶   From the beach, turn left at the minor road along a tarred path for some 1.2 miles (2 km), passing Insh Church and crossing the Spey Bridge (NH 835 056) towards Kincraig village. (On 19th century maps, before the bridge, this is indicated as a ferry crossing point, with Kincraig seemingly deriving its name from a house to the north).

ⓘ **Insh Church** is situated on the edge of Loch Insh. There are no church records prior to 1838 but it is thought that the church was renovated extensively in 1780. The church has an ancient bronze bell thought to symbolise the flame of the Holy Spirit, supported by wrought-iron doves which make reference to the doves of St Columba. The original Manse house, now Insh Guest House, was designed by Thomas Telford.

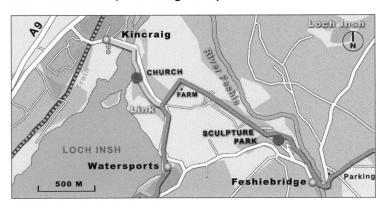

▶ Section 7
Kincraig to Aviemore

- **Distance:** 10.5 miles (16.8 km)
- **Terrain summary:** This final leg of the journey uses well established forest tracks for the most part which provide glimpse views of the Cairngorm foothills. From Feshiebridge, the forestry track ascends steadily until you finally leave the regular plantation on a smaller footpath through ancient bog forest. After passing the island castle of Loch an Eilein, the route then descends towards Aviemore through forests and open fields, leaving only a short walk to town by a pleasant cycle path to complete the journey.
- **Refreshment options:** Kincraig, Insh Watersports Centre, Rothiemurchus, Aviemore.
- **Attractions:** Fishing at Rothiemurchus, Quad biking, Sledgedog Centre, Cairngorm Ski Centre and Mountain Railway.
- **Accommodation options:** Kincraig, Feshiebridge, (Inshriach Bothy) and Aviemore.

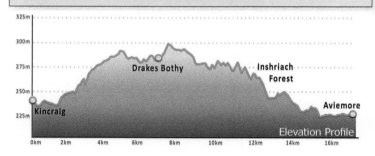

Loch an Eilein Castle.

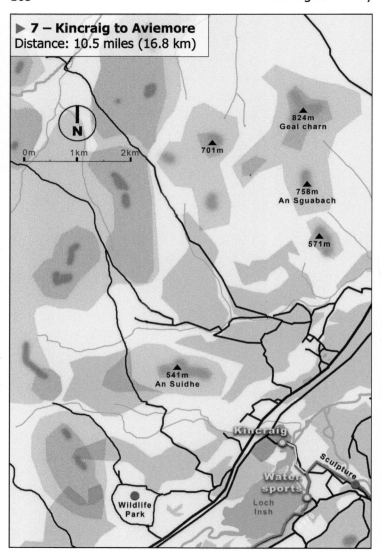

▶ 7 – Kincraig to Aviemore
Distance: 10.5 miles (16.8 km)

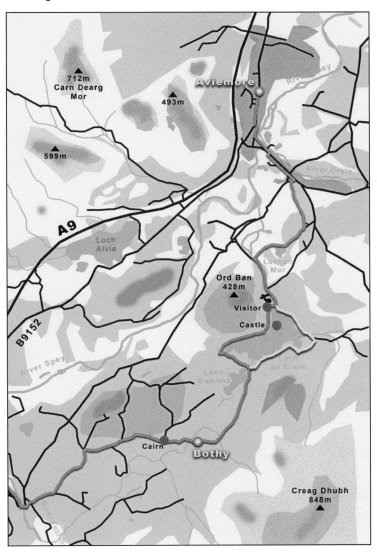

▶   From your accommodation in Kincraig, make your way back across the Spey bridge, following the Badenoch Way back around Alvie & Insh Parish Church (NH 835 053).

▶   Continue south-east back along the Badenoch Way until you arrive at the large white Invereshie Estate gates (NH 83801 05041). Turn left at the gates following the 'public footpath to Feshiebridge' sign leading towards some farm buildings. Just after the farm you arrive at a gated field (NH 839 052). Follow the track right at this point through 2 metal gates – remembering to leave them as you have found them.

▶   As the large peach-coloured Invereshie House comes into view on your right, proceed through another gate straight on as the track narrows to a well-trodden footpath (NH 841 051).

A Frank Bruce sculpture titled 'Millennium'.

ⓘ Attraction: **Frank Bruce Sculpture Park**

Situated on-route between Loch Insh and Feshiebridge is a must-see Sculpture Park displaying the thought-provoking sculptures of the late Frank Bruce. They were created using local timber and stone and depict the concepts and visions of a man who felt unable to express himself through the written or spoken word due to his debilitating dyslexia. The park is maintained as a memorial to Frank Bruce with the trail passing seamlessly through his wonderfully carved and chiselled figures. The quality of artwork on display makes this park a must-see attraction and well worth visiting in any weather. Entry to the park is free and there is a picnic area situated in the gardens. Visit **www.frank-bruce.org.uk** for further info.

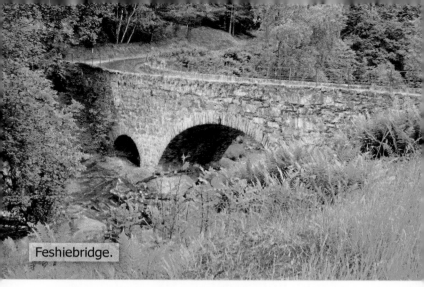

Feshiebridge.

▶ The footpath traverses a high wooded bund as the River Feshie now comes into view on the left. After passing some buildings on your right you soon arrive at the gate signalling the Frank Bruce Sculpture Trail (NH 845 048). You can explore the park by taking the access gate in the wall to your right, or continue straight on to bypass.

▶ At the east end of the sculpture trail, turn left downhill towards the public carpark (NH 848 046). Rejoin the path at the far end of the carpark as it follows the river upstream towards Feshiebridge (NH 849 046).

▶ After a short while you pass a picnic bench and arrive at Feshiebridge (NH 851 043), an old stone crossing with impressive torrent below. Another example of a Grade B-listed Bridge from the later part of the 18th century, this high single span rubble bridge with side flood arch is thought to have been originally built for military operations in the area.

▶   Exit via stile next to the orange and yellow waymarker, turning sharply left at the minor road junction, crossing the old bridge as the road bends right, turning sharply left.

▶   After 40 m, just before the white cottage with beech hedging, turn right through an old timber gate, ascending through trees on a tarred track (see image opposite).

▶   At the top of this hill, known as Heather Brae, cross the minor road and enter the forest tracks though a green gate. This part of the route can be more difficult to navigate as it involves a number of forest junctions. It may help to count the number of junctions as you pass. Pass the forestry car park on your right noticing a small footpath leading off it. Continue along the main larger track which bends leftwards away from the parking area.

▶   NH 857 045 **Forest Junction 1** – Take the first left soon after the carpark which leads uphill via a much smaller track.

ⓘ   It may seem more intuitive to continue straight at this point, but missing junction 1 would take you through a maze of paths before arriving back at junction 4 (see map below).

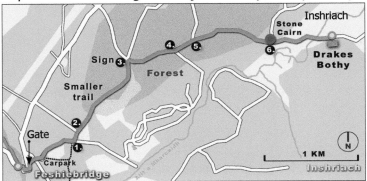

Heather Brae gate, Feshiebridge.

▶ NH 857 046, **Forest Junction 2** – As you ascend, notice a footpath turning left, continue straight on. You soon pass another waymarker indicating number 1 route.

▶ NH 862 054, **Forest Junction 3** – At this large junction go right. (Notice sign for Dalnavert left.) Turning right, you are soon presented with fine glimpse views of the Cairngorms through the trees as the track contours east. (Basically, go straight, avoiding any further turns until leaving the forest at Junction 6, marked by a small rubble cairn.)

▶ NH 867 055, **Forest Junction 4** – At this junction go straight on via the left hand fork, following the blue waymarker now indicating number 2. (Notice the right hand track leads downhill.)

▶ NH 869 056, **Forest Junction 5** – At this junction, continue straight on via the right hand fork (pass the waymarked track turning sharply north to your left). After continuing straight on you soon pass another blue waymarker indicating number 2.

▶ NH 877 056 **Forest Junction 6** – At this last junction on a bend, marked by a stone-pile cairn, take the right hand turn straight on, soon leaving the forest as the track narrows.

ⓘ Inshriach Nature Reserve

The route crosses land owned by Scottish Natural Heritage within the Invereshie and Inshriach National Nature Reserve, part of the wider Cairngorm National Park.

Being a unique ecosystem within the British Isles, these Caledonian Forests were formed at the end of the last ice age and are home to some of the country's rarest wildlife. Particular care is required through this area as it is home to many species of European importance sensitive to disturbance. For example, the area is a very important habitat for the Capercaillie, (Tetrao urogallus – a large Grouse-like bird) which is a European Protected Species – with UK numbers now thought to be less than 2000. Other rarities include the Crested Tit, the Scottish Crossbill and the illusive Pine Marten.

Walkers are reminded to behave with respect, keep to the path and always keep dogs under close control, especially between March and August. It is advised that walkers familiarise themselves with the principles set out in the Scottish Outdoor Access Code, especially when passing through sensitive environmental areas.

Loch Gamnha.

▶ After crossing a small timber bridge, you soon arrive at Inshriach (or Drake's) Bothy nestled in some open woodland to the right (NH 883 056).

ⓘ This is a primitive timber shelter with no sanitation and is maintained by Scottish National Heritage. Due to its location in an area designated for its conservation value it is very important that potential users are reminded that they cannot cut wood for fires and that they must be prepared to pack out human waste. This unique surrounding habitat of ancient bog forest is extremely vulnerable to fires. The adjacent Rothiemurchus Estate posts fire warnings and it is advised that camping stoves should be used with caution and only at times of low fire risk.

▶ Continuing past Drake's Bothy (NH 883 056), the path turns in a more northwards direction, crossing a small stream after 300 m through some low scrub of pine and birch. You pass a small boggy lochan on your right.

▶ As Loch Gamhna appears to your left, continue straight on with the path becoming a more substantial track.

▶ The trail to the left leads down towards Loch Gamnha (NH 892 068), a shallow loch of glacial origin meaning 'calf lake'.

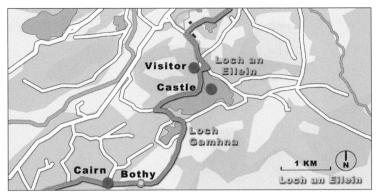

ⓘ In 1964 a forest warden on patrol around Loch Gamhna found an ancient bronze cauldron, a few metres out from the eastern shore, 300 m from the loch outflow. The cauldron, formed of bronze plates riveted together, was discovered in relatively shallow peat, suggesting that it may have been pulled up and discarded by earlier fishermen. This find prompted the search for crannog dwellings in the loch but as yet none have been discovered. (Crannogs were timber-built fortified lake villages, built on man-made islands.)

▶ There is a circular track around Loch an Eilein (see Historical Attractions p31), (meaning 'loch of the island'). Turning left around the north-west shore is slightly shorter in distance, passing the island castle and arriving at the visitor centre and car park (NH 896 083).

▶ From the visitor centre, head down to the loch and cross the loch outflow – over the footbridge to the east and turn left at the junction with the larger track. Continue past the car park on your left, going straight past the next junction on your right (NH 897 086). After 500 m turn right before the bridge, just past Milton cottage (NH894 093).

Osprey fishing at Loch Garten.

ⓘ Attraction: **Loch Garten Osprey Centre**

Ospreys have been known to nest on the walls of Loch an Eilein Castle as far back as 1863, with other early historical sightings recorded around 1881. Then in 1885 birds were known to have nested in the nearby Loch Gamhna, which connects to Loch an Eilein much like spectacle-lochs. The increasing number of tourists attracted to the castle meant nesting sites were disturbed and eggs frequently taken by collectors around this period. When a pair finally returned in 1892 they were disturbed again and left, although from 1894 to 1897 successful breeding years were again recorded at the castle. 1899 saw the last successful breeding Ospreys at Loch an Eilein but due to a severe forest fire and rival fighting, the eggs were unsuccessful. Single birds did indeed visit this part of the Rothiemurchus but remained mate-less. Since then, there have been no reports of any Ospreys returning to the ancestral eyrie at Loch an Eilein.

Although Ospreys no longer occupy the castle walls, they do travel each year from Africa to the adjacent Abernethy Forest in early April until the end of August. Situated only a few miles east of the route, the Loch Garten Osprey Centre provides a great place to view these birds fishing and on the nest. June and July are the best months to visit where you can even watch the birds live on screens thanks to their televised monitoring system. There is usually an entrance charge to the centre but well worth a visit. Check **www.rspb.org.uk** for further info.

Historical nest location.

Lochan Mor.

▶ Continue straight on past another cottage, the path itself becoming wider. Pass Lochan Mor (Large Lochan) on your right, a man-made lily loch. At the large forked junction turn left (NH 903 099), now heading northwards towards Inverdruie soon passing a small footpath which joins from the right.

▶ Pass through the gate at the next junction, arriving at the minor road and then turn right (NH 901 108).

▶ As you arrive at the Rothiemurchus Visitor Centre, turn left along a cycle track, following the B9152. Cross the road, following the cycle track. At the Rothiemurchus Fishing Centre, the route joins a forest trail swinging westwards.

▶ Cross an old metal bridge over the Spey for the final time (NH 894 117), turning right just beyond onto Dalfaber Road. Pass the Old Bridge Inn Bunkhouse and follow the pavement towards Aviemore (meaning 'big hill face'). Turn left under the railway bridge, finally arriving on Grampian Road. Turn right along Grampian road for 400 m past the shops until you arrive at the Speyside Way's southern end marker (NH 895 128) – the finishing point of the journey.

ⓘ Attraction:
Rothiemurchus Estate

The last section of the route utilises various trails managed and maintained by the Rothiemurchus Estate. If you have time, it's well worth checking out the various activities the estate has on offer. Something I've always fancied is their Tree-Zone adventure playground. This tree-top assault course is situated really close to the route on its approach to Aviemore and looks well worth a visit.

Rothiemurchus is a great place to explore whether you like a quiet ramble through the beautiful forest, around the stunning lochs, or simply enjoying the fresh air and marvelling at its stunning scenery. Visit the Rothiemurchus website for a full list of the activities on offer: **www.rothiemurchus.net**.

Approaching Aviemore.

Time to reflect and make a difference:

Congratulations on having successfully completed the East Highland Way and having traversed some of Scotland's most pristine wilderness. It's worth taking some time to reflect on our native species and consider what we can do to help protect, conserve and maintain them through these troubled times. **What we can do to help?:**

---

1 – Look out for Red Squirrels:

Sightings of red squirrels can be reported online by visiting **www.redsquirrelsofthehighlands.co.uk**, an organisation which goes a long way in helping to preserve and protect the species. It is just as important to record any sightings of non-native grey squirrels. So far the story in the Highlands is a very positive one as grey squirrels have yet to find a route north. Coupled with deforestation and squirrelpox, the grey could spell the end for the native reds unless new ways to control this man-made problem are found (see p34).

---

2 – Watch out for Wildcats:

A significant problem with Scottish Wildcat conservation is that very little is known about their population size or distribution. It is estimated that less than 400 pure Wildcats and around 3500 hybrid Wildcats live in the Highlands. Numerous surveys are being planned in the near future to clarify the situation, but in the mean time, eye witness reports give conservationists a great general indication of where Wildcats live across Scotland. So if you have seen a Wildcat on the route, can describe it in detail or supply a picture and give an accurate location of the sighting, then it's well worth emailing the Scottish Wildcat Association at **sightings@scottishwildcats.co.uk**.

ⓘ Wildcat Identification:
– Mostly brown black tiger-stripe markings.
– Dorsal stripe ends at base of tail.
– Very thick tail with a blunt end.
– Black rings along tail with large black tip.

3 – Butterfly Conservation:

Butterflies are beautiful insects that are a joy to observe as well as identify. It's possible to find up to 27 species along the length of the route so it's well worth keeping a look out. Records of all butterflies are important, even of the most common species. Up-to-date information on the locations of butterfly colonies can help conservationists best target the areas of most concern. All you need to do is send in your records to a BNM (Butterflies for the New Millennium) Co-ordinator. It's important to provide details of which butterflies you saw and roughly how many, as well as location, date and grid reference if possible.

You can get further sighting information and a very useful identification guide from Butterfly Conservation Scotland at **www.butterfly-conservation.org**.

ⓘ **Peacock Butterfly**
Feeding on nettles and caterpillars, it colonised the Cairngorms from the south in the mid 1990s and is now a common garden butterfly.

Adults are often seen in spring but their offspring can been seen in much larger numbers from July to September.

4 – Sightings of Hen Harriers

A campaign to record Hen Harrier numbers and distribution has been launched by the Cairngorms National Park Authority. These expert predators have been worryingly persecuted as they prey on heavily prized game birds such as grouse. The RSPB lists the Hen Harrier as a 'red' status species, meaning it is threatened and populations have suffered severe recent declines in numbers. Their campaign to tag and release birds is in an effort to understand and track their movements and distribution. If you spot Hen Harriers during your trip, it's well worth recording the location and getting in touch with the National Park Authority to report your sighting at **www.cairngorms.**

5 – The decline of Water Voles

Our native Water Vole, once abundant throughout the UK, has undergone a catastrophic national decline. It's thought that over the last 50 years 94% of our Water Vole sites have now become devoid of these endangered creatures. However, it's a different story in the Cairngorms, which is now recognised as a nationally important stronghold for successful breeding populations. One reason for their dramatic decline has been the introduction of alien Mink species some years ago. Work continues to create a 'mink-free' zone in the area, allowing Water Voles to re-populate and colonise this ancient wilderness once again. By recording your sightings, conservationists have a better chance of monitoring the Voles' progress and defending their habitat against Mink (the Voles are often mistaken for Brown Rats). To email your sightings visit the National Park Authority website at **www.cairngorms.co.uk**.

6 — Help the Capercaillie

The charismatic and intriguing Capercaillie is endangered and needs our help. From a population high in the 1970s of 20,000, only about 1,000 birds were recorded at the turn of the century. The risk of losing the bird completely is now a reality, due to various factors including the erection of deer fences which cause these low-flying birds no end of headaches. The Capercaillie's breeding display ground, or 'lek' as it's known, showcases the bird's majestic character, placing its enduring image in the Scottish psyche as the king of the pinewoods. Its name translates from the Gaelic 'capull collie', literally meaning 'horse of the woods', a reflection of the bird's impressive bulk.

They are most frequently sighted crashing through the low-hanging branches of dense pinewood, reaching speeds of up to 40mph, with an unusual 'klip-klopping' call, also accounting for its equestrian comparison. The RSPB are campaigning for funding to help protect these birds throughout the area. If you wish to donate you should check the RSPB website for more information at **www.rspb.org.uk**.

ⓘIdentification:
Although normally thought of as black in colour, the breast feathers are a fantastic dark metallic green. The red colouration, which can often be mistaken for feathers, is actually a bright red spot of naked skin above each eye.

Connect with the Speyside Way

After completing the East Highland Way in Aviemore, why not try the established and well marked Speyside Way. In contrast, you'll find this route easier underfoot as it passes over gentler, more agricultural terrain. The route generally follows the valley of the River Spey, passing some of the distilleries that produce Speyside single malts. The final five miles from Spey Bay to Buckie follow the coastline.

The route begins in Aviemore town centre and ends at Cluny Square in Buckie, some 65.5 miles (104.7 km) to the north. There is a spur leading off the main route to Tomintoul bringing the total distance up to 80 miles (122 km). An extension of the route from Aviemore to Newtonmore is currently being planned. This extension would lengthen the total route by 21.6 miles (34.8 km), roughly following the route of the River Spey towards Newtonmore. Visit the official Speyside Way website for further route info: **www.moray.gov.uk/area/speyway/webpages/index.htm**.

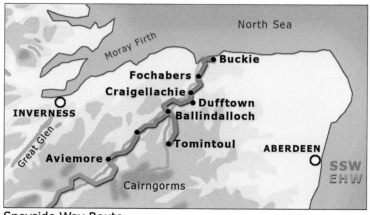

Speyside Way Route

185

Photo credits:

Anne Robertson – 139. **Ann Langan** – 179. **André van Aken** – 1, 2, 26, 69, 70, 76B, 96, 98, 123, 126, 132B, 133. **Badenoch and Strathspey Conservation Group** (www.bscg.org.uk) – 150. **David Langan** – (www.thenorthlight.co.uk). 12, 18, 21, 22, 44, 49, 52, 58, 71, 72, 73, 74, 76T, 77, 78, 83, 84, 86, 91, 92, 101, 110, 122, 124, 136, 142, 151, 154T, 155, 162, 170, 174, 184T, 184B. **Douglas Berndt** – 152, 181, 182. **Ewan & Fiona Fraser** (www.fraserbalgowan.com) – 129, 130. **Highland Folk Museum** – 140. **James Dean Shepherd** – 48, 50. **Jamie Galbraith** – I, 109, 111, 167. **Jamie Robertson** (www.jackthehat.co.uk) – 32. **John Andrews** – 41, 42. **Julie Deans & Steve Higson** (www.geminiwalks.com) – III, 7, 28, 29, 131, 132T, 138, 146, 147, 148. **Kevin Langan** – 15, 24, 30, 31, 41, 53, 54, 55, 56, 63, 64, 65, 65T, 66, 68, 79, 80, 82, 89, 90, 93, 94, 94T, 95, 97, 99, 102, 105, 107, 108, 114, 134, 154B, 156, 158, 165, 169, 171, 175, 176. **Laurie Langan** – 34, 35, 37, 38. **Kirsty McClure** – back cover B. **Mark Andrews** – 36, 178. **Paul R Byrne** – 103, 104, front cover. **Penny Weir** (www.frank-bruce.org.uk) – 166R. **Pete Walkden** – 173. **Sean McLachlan** – 19, 23, 25, 27, 61, 67, 81, 106T, 106B, 112, 118, 121T, 121B, 159, 166L. **Steve Carter** (www.pinemarten.org.uk) –.39, 40. **Stuart Campbell** – 100.

Front cover – Ardverikie Estate, Lochan na h-Earba
Title Page – Strath an Eilich, by Laggan
Back cover – Rothiemurchus, by Aviemore

Acknowledgements:

The author wishes to thank Ardverikie Estate, Arran Brown, Badenoch & Strathspey Conservation Group, Cameron McNeish, David Langan, David Meldrum, Ewan & Fiona Fraser, Fiona Dodds, Gus Jones, The Highland Folk Museum, Iona Malcolm, Jamie Galbraith, John Anderson, Joy Dunlop, Julie Deans, Kate Marshall, Katie Langan, Kirsty McClure, Laggan Forest Trust, Mark Stephen, Richard Patterson, Rio Tinto Alcan, Rob Whitson, Sean McLachlan, Steve Higson, Tim Gray and The Frank Bruce Sculpture Trust for their input and support.

 www.easthighlandway.com

ⓘ Spey Viaduct, Garmouth:
The Speyside Way route passes this stunning viaduct, built in 1886.

ⓘ Dufftown Distillery:
Strathspey is world renowned for its high concentration of single malt distilleries, the oldest of which dates back to 1786.

Luath Press Limited
committed to publishing well written books worth reading

LUATH PRESS takes its name from Robert Burns, whose little collie Luath (*Gael.,* swift or nimble) tripped up Jean Armour at a wedding and gave him the chance to speak to the woman who was to be his wife and the abiding love of his life. Burns called one of 'The Twa Dogs' Luath after Cuchullin's hunting dog in Ossian's *Fingal.* Luath Press was established in 1981 in the heart of Burns country, and now resides a few steps up the road from Burns' first lodgings on Edinburgh's Royal Mile.
Luath offers you distinctive writing with a hint of unexpected pleasures.

Most bookshops in the UK, the US, Canada, Australia, New Zealand and parts of Europe either carry our books in stock or can order them for you. To order direct from us, please send a £sterling cheque, postal order, international money order or your credit card details (number, address of cardholder and expiry date) to us at the address below. Please add post and packing as follows: UK – £1.00 per delivery address; overseas surface mail – £2.50 per delivery address; overseas airmail – £3.50 for the first book to each delivery address, plus £1.00 for each additional book by airmail to the same address. If your order is a gift, we will happily enclose your card or message at no extra charge.

Luath Press Limited
543/2 Castlehill
The Royal Mile
Edinburgh EH1 2ND
Scotland
Telephone: 0131 225 4326 (24 hours)
Fax: 0131 225 4324
email: sales@luath.co.uk
Website: www.luath.co.uk

Index: